Britain by Bicycle

Britain by Bicycle

The RALEIGH Guide to
Cycle Touring

Rob Hunter

Weidenfeld and Nicolson
London

Britain is known to be the most flourishing
and excellent, most renowned and famous island
of the whole world.

WILLIAM CAMDEN

Illustration Acknowledgments

Most of the photographs have been supplied by the British Tourist
Authority but a few have been reproduced by kind permission of
the following: *J. Allan Cash* frontispiece, 57, 81, 82–3, 89 *above,*
96–7, 100, 117, 118–9, 125 *above,* 132–3, 146–7, 153, 154–5,
174–5, 177, 184, 185, 195, back jacket *(hardback)*; *S.J. Dobell* 201
above; *Syndication International* 140; *Chris Webb* 9.

The maps and diagram are by Heather Sherratt.

Published in Great Britain in 1985 by
George Weidenfeld & Nicolson Limited
91 Clapham High Street
London SW4 7TA

ISBN 0 297 78630 X (cased)
ISBN 0 297 78631 8 (paper)

Phototypeset by Deltatype, Ellesmere Port, S. Wirral
Printed in Great Britain by
Butler & Tanner Ltd., Frome and London

Contents

High Burnham Beeches, a forest owned by the City of London.

Introduction

People will tell you that mass tourism, the car, the jet plane, the hotel chain, have brought the world to our doorsteps and killed that sense of excitement and adventure that used to come from travel. That's what they say, but don't you believe it! What matters today is not just where you travel, but how. Travel by car or aircraft, stay in a high-rise hotel, and the world, I grant you, is much of a muchness, but why travel like that? What is the point of it, and where is the fun?

I must straight away plead guilty to being a supporter of the cause of fun. Those who wish to join me and discover, or rediscover, that sense of fun and adventure that comes from true travel need do no more than buy a bike.

Beginnings, even in bicycling, are never easy. I started cycle touring the hard way, buying a cycle and setting off across France and Spain down the Pilgrim Road to Compostela in Spain. In the previous thirty years I had probably cycled no more than ten miles. It took me a month to get to Compostela, and there were times on that long, hard, hot journey when I felt that I was learning more about cycle touring than I really wanted to know. Travelling by bike is addictive, though, and since that time my bike and I have been on many long tours, at home and abroad. With luck we shall continue to do so for many years to come, but having had the experience of learning the hard way, I hope that this book will enable the reader to start cycle touring with greater ease and fewer mistakes.

The bicycle is a marvellous invention, ideal for the adventurous traveller, a device for going places. It has clear advantages over all other forms of locomotion. Buy a bike and the most remote corners of the world can come within reach, the distances spilling past at fifty miles a day or more. Bicycles are patient, simple steeds, accepting heavy loads without complaint, happy with a little oil, air and grease, giving little trouble if you treat them well. Inanimate objects they may be, but one soon feels fond of them. Cycling is less exhausting than walking, less exclusive and less expensive than motoring, less trouble than horse riding. As a final bonus, it gets you fit.

This is a book about cycle touring in Britain, the country of my birth. I make that point because, although I am a travel writer, I earn my living for the most part by travelling overseas. This book, and my bicycle, have given me a chance to renew contacts with my own country; to visit again or for the first time some favoured places in the various regions and counties, and to see such places as they should be seen, at a gentle pace, on minor roads, with plenty of time to stop, stare, talk to the locals and enjoy the view. This, indeed, is perhaps the greatest advantage of the bicycle; it gets you where you want to go quite quickly, but it gives you time to enjoy the journey – the perfect combination.

This book is divided into three parts. The first covers the hardware: the cycles, the equipment, the essential touring extras, the practical side of cycle touring. The second deals with clothing and fitness, and the practical elements of planning and riding a tour. Good planning is the basis of an enjoyable and successful cycle tour, for you must know where you are going, and plot attractive ways to get there. Straying off the route may mean nothing to the motorist, but unnecessary extra distance can mean long hours in the saddle to the cyclist.

The greater part of the book consists of twenty cycle tours, usually on minor roads, to and through the varied regions of Britain. These tours vary in length from one to three weeks, and finish with the Great British Bike Ride, the End-to-End, from Land's End to John O' Groats, which most British cyclists, or those who come here from overseas, will want to attempt at some time.

The author outside St Bartholomew Church, Fingest.

I must emphasize that the book is not simply a route guide, full of directions; these already exist in plenty and a list of them will be found in the bibliography. It is a *tour* guide, and aims to provide the traveller – who may not at this moment even be a cyclist – with the encouragement and motivation to get on a cycle and discover the country in a new, fresh way.

Any cycle tour is all the better for a theme: to ride along the coast, to see the East Anglian cathedrals, to ride from end to end or west to east. If there is an overall theme, it is history, partly because I love history, and partly because Britain is an historic country. I have also used these tours to visit places I have always wanted to see, and only regret the many places which, because of time or distance, I have had to leave out.

The routes offered should first be traced on a map, but they need not be followed too exactly. Travellers should never be bound to a rigid itinerary, and cycling is a sport for freedom lovers.

Having established that this is a book for travel lovers, may I say that I am not a committed, obsessive cyclist. I cycle because I enjoy it, and my ignorance of the more arcane aspects of gears and cogs and levers is profound. This has not prevented me – nor will it you – from planning and enjoying some splendid British tours on that most delightful of transports, the bicycle.

ROB HUNTER
1985

The Touring Bicycle

The two-wheeled velocipede is the animal which is to supersede everything else.
The Velocipedist, 1869

Britain is the home of cycle touring. Other countries, notably France and Belgium, may produce the great racing cyclists of the world, and some countries such as Holland and India may put the bicycle to more regular daily use, but when it comes to using the cycle as a machine for going places, Britain leads the field.

By current estimates more than three million people in Britain already have a bike, but it may not be one designed or even suitable for extended cycle touring. Cycles can be broadly divided into three categories, racing, commuting and touring, and while there is some overlap between the types the true touring machine is a separate breed, with unique characteristics. It is possible to go touring, for a while and at a pinch, on almost any kind of bicycle, but those who get bitten by the touring bug will find the whole experience less strenuous and more fun on a well-made, specially designed and properly equipped touring machine.

First, a note of warning: a glance through the letter pages of the cycling magazines will soon reveal that some cyclists are deeply committed to their machines, and have set views on how a touring machine should be assembled. Almost every item, from brake blocks to spoke meshing, from seat angle to the brazing of frame joints, is argued with passion and considerable technical knowledge, and also with a certain degree of paranoia. Those cyclists who rave on about their opinions fail to notice that others are equally committed to an entirely different point of view, and will deploy similar, if different, arguments to support their case. Those who come fresh to cycle touring may find all this sound and fury a little alarming, even somewhat off-putting. After listening patiently to the clamour for several years, I have come to the opinion that those who like the technical side of cycles are entitled to their pleasures, but those of us who simply enjoy cycling have nothing at all to worry about. Those who invest in a good, well-designed machine will have made an investment in enjoyment. It certainly pays to know how to maintain the cycle, and all cycle tourists should be able to carry out simple repairs, but that apart, there is nothing to worry about in the standard 10-, 12- or 15-speed touring bicycle on which this book is based. As long as its design incorporates certain essential elements, such a machine can take the rider anywhere he or she wants to go.

This chapter looks at the design and construction of the cycle-touring machine, and tells you where to buy it, how to equip and adapt it, and how to maintain it. A good machine will give you years of trouble-free riding, so it pays to buy a suitable machine, equip it for touring with a few advisable extras, and learn how to look after it.

The Touring Machine

After excluding racing models and the three-geared sit-up-and-beg boneshakers from the categories listed above, if you want a touring machine you have three choices. First, you can go off on your present bike if you have one, and learn to cope with any inherent limitations (see p. 27 for how to upgrade it). Second, and at the other extreme, you can go to a specialist cycle builder, explain your requirements, and rely on that firm to design and build a touring cycle to match those criteria. Hand-built cycles are expensive, though, and it would be as well to wait a few years and build up some experience before investing in a hand-built touring machine.

The third alternative, and my advice to those who do not already have a cycle, or have one which is clearly unsuitable for touring, is to buy an off-the-peg touring machine and adapt it to fit. This is not a racer. I am often asked 'Do you have a racer?', a racer to most people being any bike with drop handlebars, and therefore complicated. My bike *does* have drop handlebars, but it is a touring machine with distinct, if subtle, differences from a racing machine. The traveller requires a touring machine (see diagram opposite) and, even at a basic level, such a machine will have a long wheelbase, at least ten gears, a pannier rack, drop handlebars and mudguards as the most visible elements. If it has these, you are looking at the right kind of bicycle, but to get the right cycle *for you* may take a little longer.

Buying a Touring Cycle

Many shops sell cycles, but the only sensible place to buy one is in a proper cycle store, which in Britain is one registered with the NACT (National Association of Cycle Traders). As a general rule, good touring machines cannot be found in those shops which also sell toys

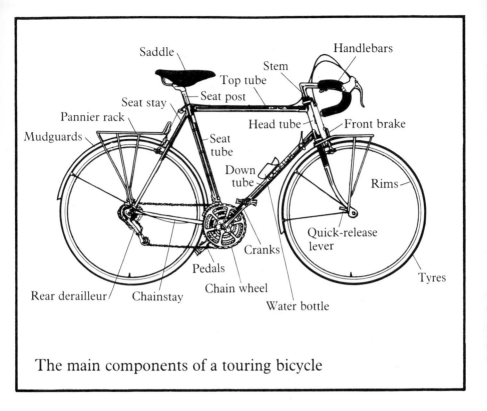

The main components of a touring bicycle

or electrical goods. NACT outlets stock a good range of machines, carry spares, maintain a service department, and have competent, well-informed staff. More important, NACT retailers are cyclists who care about cycling. They will give you good advice, adjust the machine to fit, and take it back for further adjustment and servicing after you have ridden it for a hundred miles or so. Most towns of any size will have at least one NACT retailer, whose addresses can be found from advertisements in the cycling magazines (see Bibliography), or in your local Yellow Pages.

Take your time when buying a cycle. Visit the shop several times and talk to the staff. Once the choice has narrowed to one or two machines, talk to someone who owns one. Most good cycle shops are like a clubhouse to the local cyclists and they all love discussing their machines. On a Saturday morning, the crowd outside is a useful group to linger with and pick up good advice.

It is possible, if you know what you want, to buy a good secondhand machine via the local press or cycling magazines. If the machine is any good you will have to be quick, for bargains are snapped up quickly, but obviously any secondhand machine, however much of a bargain it might appear, has to be regarded with caution. Has it been damaged or (even worse) stolen? Does the owner have proof of purchase, (which he or she should have if the machine is fairly new)? How long has he or she owned it, how many miles has it covered, why is it being sold? Examine the frame carefully. Then go for a ride on the machine, taking your hands off the handlebars to see if the frame or forks are distorted. If the bike's wheels don't track properly, don't buy the bike.

Take your time making up your mind, for a good touring bike currently (1985) costs between £150 and £300. There are many discounts available, but although cycle prices have stayed remarkably stable prices are unlikely to fall, and that sort of expenditure deserves serious thought and sound advice before you part with your money.

One final piece of advice: always buy the best machine you can afford. Those who settle for something less will inevitably become dissatisfied after a short while, and having to change one machine for a better one always costs you more in the end. When buying a bicycle, you get exactly what you pay for.

Frame

The frame (see page 13) is the heart of the touring bicycle. There are basically two types of frame, the male or 'diamond' frame, with top tube (or crossbar), and the female or 'mixte' frame, with two thinner, sloping crossbars. More and more women cyclists are in fact opting for the diamond design, which is stronger and, if properly constructed from the correct materials, gives a more flexible frame and therefore an easier, more responsive ride.

Cycle frames are built from steel, or steel-manganese alloy tubing. All the best frames are built from this special cycle tubing and are usually double butted; the Reynolds 531 manganese-molybdenum, as used on the Classic 15 Raleigh tourer, is the finest frame tubing available. Double-butted tubing is thin in the middle, for lightness, and thicker at the ends, where the stress falls, for strength. Apart from the material, the cost of a frame usually depends on the amount of double-butted tubing it contains, so that a moderately priced frame may have only the main tubes – top, down, and seat tube – double butted, while a more expensive frame may be double butted throughout. Double butted tubing is light, strong, and well worth paying for, so buy as much of it as you can afford.

Whether the frame tubes should be 'lugged', that is, fitted into sockets at the joints, is debatable. It is probably a matter of personal preference, but I prefer my frames lugged. If you choose an unlugged frame, then check the brazing, where the tubes join, carefully. Poor brazing creates a weak joint and rough brazing indicates sloppy workmanship.

Pay attention to the wheelbase, the forks, and the chainstay. The wheelbase is the distance between the front and rear fork sockets, or drop-outs, and on a touring cycle this distance should be at least 41 ins, or even a little more. Touring cycles, as you can see at a glance, tend to be longer than racing models. This feature is enhanced by the front forks, which are raked forward from the vertical by about 2 ins, a feature known as fork rate.

The chainstays, between the crank and the rear forks, should be around 17 ins on a tourer. Touring frame chainstays are also longer than those on racing machines, and this extra length offers various advantages: the chain angle between chain set and rear cogs is reduced, and wider gear ratios are therefore possible; pannier racks can be more central on the frame, which helps balance; and your feet can turn the cranks without your heels hitting the pannier bags.

Frame Size

This is critical, and depends on the size of the rider. Obtaining a frame as close to the correct size as possible is a first essential when buying a touring machine, and an important step towards ensuring a comfortable fit. As a general rule, the frame size will be that of your inner leg measurement less 9 ins. This yardstick holds good for diamond frame and mixte machines. On a diamond frame machine, you should be able to straddle the top tube comfortably with your feet flat on the ground. Standard frame sizes for adult machines are from 21 ins (54 cm) to 25 ins (64 cm). Cycle measurements are still expressed in a mixture of metric and imperial units.

Once the correct frame size has been established, minor adjustments can be made to the fit by raising or lowering the saddle or handlebars, but only within strict limits. For safety's sake, there must be plenty of post left in both the seat and head tube.

Wheels

Next in importance to the frame are the wheels. Indeed, when it comes to upgrading a cycle, buying good, well-built wheels is the first point to consider, as nothing will contribute as much to the successful completion of an extended tour. Wheels are crucial because all your effort, via the cranks, chain and cogs, is expended on making them turn. The lighter and more responsive they are, the easier this task will be, and the effort required will be that much less. Whatever else you may skimp on, don't do it on the wheels.

Wheels are constructed from three separate components, rims, spokes and hubs, whose overall aim is to combine strength and lightness. Popular diameters are 27 and 26 ins. The rims should be of aluminium alloy. Steel rims are heavier but not stronger and are prone to rust. Modern alloys offer advantages on both these points and, when allied to the correct brake block, offer improved braking power.

Wheel spoking is another area for debate: opinions are divided between 36 and 40 spokes in the wheel, and on the possible gauge of the spoke. Personally I think 36 spokes, 14 gauge, quite adequate. The interleaving or meshing of the spokes is also a subject of controversy, but treble meshing is the most generally accepted type.

Spokes are usually made in chrome-steel of 14–16 mm gauge. It is possible to buy double butted spokes, which some cyclists prefer, maintaining that they are both lighter and stronger than straight gauge, but unless you are considering a hand-built machine with all the trimmings, straight gauge spokes are perfectly adequate.

The hubs should have the correct number of holes to match the spokes, but it does not really matter if they are the high, wide-flange type, or the small, low-flange variety. This is a matter of personal choice, and I have accepted either, on different machines, without noticing any significant difference. The hubs should be the quick-release type, so that you can release the wheel from the frame simply by flicking a lever. Some cycles only have quick-release on the front hubs, but it is so useful when mending a puncture or removing a wheel for air travel that it should be fitted to both wheels.

Apart from having strong, light components, it is essential that the wheel is well built. Wheel building is an art, and a good wheel builder, who can construct and true a wheel to fine limits, is worth his weight in gold. A poorly built or badly trued wheel will give you a poor ride and be a constant source of trouble. If you suffer from continual spoke breaking have the wheel rebuilt.

Tyres and Tubes

Tyres, or covers as cyclists call them, come in two types – the light sew-ups found on racing machines, and the stiff, wire-rimmed type with a heavy tread pattern, ideal for touring. Tourists should choose wire-on tyres, 27 or 26 ins in diameter, $1\frac{1}{2}$ or $1\frac{1}{4}$ ins in width. The other popular size is 700 cm, which is marginally smaller than the 27 × $1\frac{1}{4}$ ins, and they are not compatible. Most cyclists carry a spare cover, in case the one they are using gets damaged and cannot be replaced quickly.

Inner tubes should have either Presta or Schrader high-pressure valves – but not both on the same cycle. Make sure your pump will fit the tyre valve.

Gears

Gearing is another great subject for debate among cyclists, but if the truth were aired as often as the opinions are, once again it would have to be admitted that it is a matter of personal choice. The 'correct' gearing depends on so many factors: the weight of the load carried, the terrain, the fitness of the rider, and the daily distances; no cyclist can afford to be dogmatic about gearing, although many are. However, here are some general guidelines on touring gears.

For historical reasons, gearing ratios are expressed in inches, and the ratios are calculated from the following formula –

$$\frac{\text{No. of teeth on front sprocket}}{\text{No. of teeth on rear sprocket}} \times \text{wheel size} = \text{gearing in inches}$$

Therefore $\frac{52}{14} \times 27$ ins $= 100.2$ ins – a high gear

The cycle tourist needs ratios that step down evenly, without too much duplication, giving a wide choice that can cope with all sorts of terrain, and lend a helping hand when the wind blows relentlessly from the front. To give three further examples from the Raleigh range, the following are the ratios for the Classic 15, the Record Ace 12 and the Royal 10 (T=teeth):

Classic 15

30T: 58–48–41–34–29 ins
40T: 77–64–54–45–39 ins
50T: 96–79–68–56–48 ins

The Classic 15, with 15 gears, is designed for the serious cyclist, so it is reasonable to assume that a serious cyclist cycles a lot and has strong legs. Therefore a top of 96 is not excessive, and a low of 29 very useful. There is only one direct duplication – 48.

Record Ace 12

42T: 81–71–63–54–47–41 ins
52T: 100–88–78–67–59–50 ins

The Record Act 12 is a training-touring machine, a hybrid between the tourer and the racer, built to high standards. The top gear is 100 and the bottom 41 – a trifle high for loaded touring.

Royal 10

36T: 69–57–47–37–30 ins
50T: 96–79–64–52–42 ins

The Royal 10 is a 10-speed cycle, and this type of gearing is the choice of most cycle tourists. This machine has nice ratios of 96–30 ins, well stepped down, with no duplication. Not surprisingly, the Royal 10 is a popular touring machine.

Calculate the ratios how you will, some close ratios, or a duplication, are almost impossible to avoid. The best you can hope for is to reduce the overlap to a minimum, and obtain the most suitable gears (for you) at either end of the spectrum.

In practice, the ideal gear ratios for any individual rider are very hard to come by. Because of excessive chain angle, using the outer front ring to the inner rear ring, and vice versa, should be avoided, so the 10-gear cycle has eight effective gears and the 12- and 15-gear cycles are similarly restricted.

When buying the cycle, note the number of teeth in the front and rear cogs and work out the ratios, unless these are given in the specification. On an off-the-peg cycle, the top and bottom ratios will almost invariably be too high, a fact which generations of cycle tourists have continued to marvel at. However, there is no point in changing the gears until you have ridden the cycle for some while, and decided which ratios are best suited to your own particular requirements. It is also worth mentioning that I rode my first off-the-peg Raleigh Carlton Corsair all the way to Spain with standard gears, and no trouble whatsoever. I may have puffed a little on the Pyrenees, but I got to the top just the same. A well assorted range, from a top of around 85–90 ins to a bottom of around 30–27 ins, is about right.

Finally, although this book is based on the popular 10-speed machine, it is possible to buy cycles with 3, 5, 10, 12, 15, even 18 gears. Three-speed machines are not at all suitable for touring, and 5-speeds barely adequate. Fifteen speeds, with a third ring on the front, are very popular on the Continent and in the USA, and they are my personal choice, while the 18-speed (three front rings, six rear cogs) seems a trifle excessive. For all popular purposes, the 10-, 12- or 15-speed touring bike is the perfect machine.

The gears are changed by a system of levers and wire cables. The gear levers can be set in various places, at the handlebar ends, on the top tube, or on the down tube, which is the most popular position, though here again where they go is a matter of personal preference.

The gears will only change when the cranks and cogs are turning and, unlike a motor car, there is no fixed position for the gear lever, so that changing gear calls for fine adjustment. To achieve a smooth gear change takes a little practice. Remember to change down to a low gear when stopping, as it makes pulling away again that much easier.

Cranks and Chainsets

The cranks turn the chainset, which turns the chain, which turns the rear cogs and thus the rear wheel. The whole mechanism is sometimes referred to as the power train, or drive train.

The crank arms, which hold the pedals to the chain wheel, should be made of alloy and cotterless – in other words, they should be part of the whole chainset and not simply secured to it with a strong bolt or cotter pin. Such assemblies still exist, but alloy cotterless chainsets are by far the most popular.

The length of the crank is important because it acts as a lever to the chainset, and the longer the lever, the more effort the legs deploy. The practicalities of cycle engineering – like the fact that too long a crank will hit the ground on the corners – limits the length of the crank, and the 170 mm crank is the one most preferred on modern touring bicycles. Chainsets are also in alloy, have to be strong as well as light, and are fixed to the frame through the bottom bracket. Servicing the bottom bracket calls for regular attention and fine adjustment, for the crank and chainset are exposed to spray and road grit and get a great deal of wear and abrasion.

Pedals

Touring pedals should be of the metal rat-trap or quill variety, fitted with toe-clips and straps. Cyclists who have never used them before may find toe-clips a complication, but they hold your foot correctly on the pedal, and, by enabling you to pull up as well as push down, can add considerably to the forward momentum.

Pedals and clips should be compatible with the cyclist's shoes, and you must be able to slip out of the toe-clips in an emergency. The straps can be tightened for country riding, but it is a good idea to loosen them when entering towns or traffic, and always release at least one foot from the toe-clip before braking to a stop. Otherwise a heavy, painful sideways fall is inevitable.

Saddle

The pedals, saddle and handlebars are the cyclist's three contact points on the machine. Of the three, the saddle bears the most weight and can pose the most problems. At least in the early days, a certain amount of saddle discomfort is unavoidable.

The best saddle for the committed cyclist has a slender leather seat, and is properly broken in to the rider's shape. This takes time. The two most popular models are the leather Brooks B17 Standard, and the recently introduced Madison Anatomic, which is leather-covered and has small pads to soften the pressure on the pelvic bones. In either case, a woman's saddle should be slightly wider than the man's model.

Given the importance of a comfortable ride, choosing and preparing a saddle is worth considerable attention. The Madison should fit and be fairly comfortable from the start, although you will still need to get used to it, but the Brooks, while giving the most comfortable ride once broken in, does require some preparatory treatment.

Examine a number of saddles and choose one whose leather is not too thick or stiff. Before fitting it to the bike, work into the underside large amounts of Prufide, neat's foot oil or Mars Oil, all of which can be obtained from cycle shops or saddlery shops. This process can take several evenings before the oil is absorbed and the saddle starts to soften. It still has to conform to your shape, however, and the only way to do this is to fit the saddle to the cycle and ride on it. Adjusting the saddle on the machine is also important. It should be perfectly level, or slightly forward, and level with the top of the handlebars. For the first few rides cover the saddle with a thin cloth, or wear old shorts or trousers, for the softening oil will certainly ooze out.

It will probably take five hundred miles or more of riding before the saddle is broken in and fits your shape, but a well broken-in saddle is extremely comfortable and will last the life of several machines.

Handlebars and Stems

All touring cycles should be fitted with drop handlebars, which offer a choice of riding position and are therefore far more comfortable on an extended tour. Many commuter cyclists claim not to like drop handlebars, or regard them as a racing frill, but even those tourists who rarely go 'on the drops', or the lower bars, come to swear by them after a long tour.

Drop handlebars come in various shapes and the slightly raised Randonneur bars are marginally more popular with committed tourists than the full drop racing type. The bars can be swivelled in the socket to achieve the most comfortable position. Close attention should also be paid to the stem, the brakes and the brake hoods.

The stem connects the bars to the headset. Stems come in various lengths and are one of the ways by which the rider fits the machine to his or her body length. If the reach is too long, too much weight will fall on your arms; if too short, your shoulders and back can become cramped.

Another good fore-and-aft yardstick is to sit in the saddle and swing your arms forward to the bars. If the length is correct your fingertips should rest on the handlebar top and grip it lightly. Both saddle and stem can be adjusted to get the correct fit.

After the brakes (see below) have been positioned and other adjustments made, the bars can be fitted with thick padding called Grab-On, and a mirror. Grab-On greatly reduces road shock and vibration and is a real boon to your hands on a long tour, while a mirror – the small Mirrycle is ideal – is an essential safety feature.

Brakes

Efficient braking on a bike is important, and essential to the cycle tourist who is usually riding on a loaded machine and crossing unfamiliar terrain, when steep hills and sudden stops are all part of the day. All touring machines are fitted with cable calliper-type brakes, operated by brake levers. Some cyclists favour centre-pull brakes, while others opt for side pull, but both types are efficient provided they are properly maintained and regularly adjusted.

The sharp end of the brake is the brake block, and the brake block must be compatible with the rim. Using a steel rim block on an alloy rim will damage or distort the alloy in a very short time, so, especially when buying new or spare blocks, be very sure they will suit the rims – don't just pluck them from the showcard.

The blocks need to be fitted firmly into place and aligned exactly to ensure that the maximum braking surface is applied to the rim. The brake blocks often squeal at first, but if they continue to do so check that the rim is not oily, and if not toe-in the blocks to the front by very gently bending the brake arms with a pair of pliers. Some cycles have an extra set of brake levers, usually called dual levers or safety levers. These are certainly not as efficient as the main levers and many tourists dislike them, although I find them useful.

After a few days' constant use, a new brake cable will stretch, and if the braking power is to be maintained the slack must be taken up and the brake adjusted. This adjustment is easy to carry out with a wishbone-shaped tool called a third hand, which takes up the pressure of the brake spring while the cable is tightened.

A final useful extra on the brake lever is a brake block release. This is a small lever, or arm, which allows the brakes to open wide when the cyclist has to remove the wheel, perhaps to repair a puncture, or for transit by air.

Even if fitted with dual levers, the brakes should be set so that you can reach them easily from every riding position, and if they are fitted with rubber brake hoods you gain another comfortable riding position.

Mudguards

One feature of the touring bike which is not always found on other models, and is rare on racing bikes, is mudguards. These can be in plastic or alloy, and are very handy indeed, to protect not only the rider from wet road spray, but also the machine and panniers. A mudflap on the front mudguard reduces the amount of water and grit bombarding the chain and bottom bracket, two mechanisms much prone to wear.

Pannier Racks

The final distinctive feature of the touring cycle is the pannier rack, which carries the luggage bags or panniers (although, to be absolutely precise, panniers are the rear bags). The full assembly consists of front and rear panniers plus a handlebar bag, and some cyclists include a saddlebag and carry further equipment on the top of the rear pannier rack itself.

Pannier racks, like all the other parts of the touring machine, should be strong, light and securely fitted; I use Jim Blackburn alloy carriers. There are a number of other makes available, but not every pannier rack will carry every type of pannier, although most are compatible or can be made so. Check the pannier rack carefully and regularly, tightening any bolts or screws if they seem slack. Panniers and handlebar bags are discussed further on page 41.

Lights and Reflectors

Traffic regulations require all cycles to have lights, and the lights must be in working order. There are two types available, those powered by dry-cell batteries and those powered by a dynamo. Personally, I prefer the dry-cell battery type, because although they are heavier they are more useful on a cycle camping trip, when they can be taken off the machine and used to light the tent, and I rarely cycle after dark anyway. Dynamo lamps only work when the wheels are turning, and the dynamo itself can cause wheel drag, though some modern dynamo lamps will work when the cycle has stopped.

Current regulations also insist that cycle lights shine to the side as well as to the front and rear, and it is always advisable, if only for safety's sake, to check that the lamps are working and shining brightly. Dim or broken lights create an obvious risk, and a spare bulb in the tool kit is a useful extra. All cycles should also be fitted with a reflector, and indeed anything that can attract the attention of the motorist, especially at night, is well worth using.

Warnings

Cycles are silent runners, which move much faster than most pedestrians might suppose. A bell or a horn will often come in handy and help to avoid that mutually painful collision.

Extras

So far it is only the basic touring machine that has been described – tourists need a few extras. The cycle will have pannier racks, but a plastic water bottle or two on the down tube will be essential, for cycle touring is thirsty work. Finally, don't forget a pump, kept in working order and compatible with the inner tube valves.

A Touring Specification

To summarize the points covered so far, any machine suitable for extended cycle touring should have all, or at least most, of the following characteristics and equipment:

Frame	In high-quality steel or steel alloy, such as Reynolds 531, with as much double butting as possible. Lugged joints optional.
Wheels	36 spoke, 14 gauge, alloy rims, low or high flange, quick-release hubs.
Tyres	Touring tyres, wire-on, 27 × 1¼ ins or 700 cm.
Tubes	Schrader or Presta valves.
Gears	10-speed minimum, well-spread ratios from about 85 ins to 30 ins.
Cranks and chainset	Alloy, cotterless.
Pedals	Metal quill type, fitted with toe clips.
Saddle	Leather or leather-covered. Brooks B17 standard, or Madison Anatomic.
Handlebars	Drop, Randonneur type, fitted with Grab-On padding.
Brakes	Cable brakes, centre or side pull with dual levers optional but block release device. Fitted with rubber brake hoods.

Lights	Dry cell battery type preferred. Must offer side visibility. Spare bulb advisable.
Touring extras	Mudguards Mudflap Mirrycle mirror Pannier rack Water-bottle Pump.

Check any manufacturer's specification and see how it compares. For example:

Technical Specification

Model	Raleigh Classic 15
Frame sizes	54 cm (21 ins) 57 cm ($22\frac{1}{2}$ ins) 60 cm ($23\frac{1}{2}$ ins) 64 cm (25 ins)
Frame material	Reynolds 531 double butted tubes and taper gauge stays; Sun Tour GS forged ends, Haden Royal Sovereign lugs
Frame angles	73 ins parallel
Headset	Tange CMA60
Fork	Reynolds 531 taper gauge blades with forged Vagner Crown and Sun Tour GS forged ends
Wheels	Rims – Weinmann concave section eyeletted alloy Hubs – Mallard Competition Q.R. Spokes – 146 stainless steel
Tyres	Michelin 27 × $1\frac{1}{8}$ ins Club Tourist
Mudguards	Silver, impact-resistant, twin stays at front and rear

Handlebars	Engraved Randonneur bar with deep foam grips
Stem	SR Apex forged alloy
Brakes	Weimann centrepull with quick-release levers
Derailleur	Huret titanium-bodied Duopar rear derailleur; Club AS front and power levers
Chainset	Sugino PX forged alloy, fully detachable 50/40/30T
Freewheel	Suntour PN500014–17–20–24–28T
Gear ratios	30T : 58–48–41–34–29 ins 40T : 77–64–54–45–39 ins 50T : 96–79–68–56–48 ins
Chain	Suntour Z silver
Pedals	Alloy quill
Saddle	Brooks B17 leather
Seat pin	Sakae CTP3 alloy micro adjust
Extras	Front and rear carriers – Jim Blackburn alloy Toe clips and leather straps Frame fitting inflator Bottle cage mounts Wide-angle reflector set (to BS6102/2 – not fitted)
Approx. weight	30lb (23½ ins frame)
Colour	Burgundy with silver peak head

The cyclist who owns a touring machine which matches these criteria has made a wise investment, but buying and equipping the machine correctly is only half the battle. To tour comfortably and successfully, the machine and the rider must fit. Even small differences in the fit are crucial to the rider, and a machine that has not been correctly adjusted will demand extra energy as well as causing cramp and other discomforts.

Adjusting the Fit

Choosing the correct frame size is the first step, but the machine still has to be adjusted for leg length and body size.

The leg length is correct if, with the pedal at its lowest point, you can sit in the saddle and rest your heel on the pedal with your knee straight. When the ball of your foot is on the pedal your leg will then be slightly bent, the optimum position. Adjust the saddle until this can be achieved, a task made much easier with a micro-adjusting seat pin and a patient friend.

Having got the saddle height right, pay attention yet again to setting the correct distance between saddle and handlebars. This is best done when you buy the cycle – the shop will, or should, change the stem if the one fitted is just too long to make minor adjustment possible. Sitting in the saddle, you should be able to swing your arms forward and touch the top of the bars; alternatively, with your elbow against the nose of the saddle, your outstretched fingertips should brush the rear of the bars. Apart from changing the stem, small adjustments can be made by moving the saddle forward or back. Time spent getting these positions right will not be wasted. It may seem trivial to the commuting cyclist, who gets the chance to stop and stretch at every traffic light, but on a long tour comfort is very important.

Upgrading the Cycle

Many cyclists who already have a machine may baulk at the idea of buying another one just to go cycle touring. If the machine runs well, has a good frame, is no heavier than, say, 35–40lb, and has five or more gears, it may be possible to upgrade it to an acceptable touring level. Consult the local cycle shop and consider:
1. Buying better wheels or having them rebuilt.
2. Fitting mudguards and drop handlebars, with Grab-On, etc.
3. Changing the pedals and fitting toe clips.
4. Fitting a pannier rack.
5. Gear ratios – if too high, can they be lowered?
6. Adjusting the machine to a proper fit.

If you and your existing machine can complete the annual 56-mile London to Brighton Bike Ride, reasonable tours may be possible.

Learning to Ride

Most potential cycle tourists will already be able to ride a bicycle, but riding a 10-speed machine is something different, and riding a loaded 10-speed machine is different again. On the first occasion that I rode a 10-speed bike I wobbled off into the traffic, built up a little speed, changed gear and cartwheeled into the gutter, my feet still stuck in the toe-clips; a large lorry wheel brushed past my ears, and it was all rather alarming. The cycle was wheeled back to the shop to have the forks straightened, and I invested in some cycling gloves to spare my palms from the gravel should this happen again.

If you have never ridden a 10-speed machine start with a little practice on a quiet, level road. Learn to handle the machine from both the top of the bars and the drops, as well as riding it hands off. If the machine is running true, riding hands off should be easy, but a good touring machine with a double butted frame is highly responsive. Learn to flick your feet into the toe-clips, and get into the habit of changing into a lower gear and freeing your feet from the toe clips before stopping.

Gear changing calls for delicate adjustments and a fine touch. Try to change gear without wobbling or looking down, and listen for any rough notes. The chain should run silently over the cogs but it may be necessary to adjust the front changer slightly to achieve this. Change gear smoothly, one cog at a time, and get into the habit of doing so early on the hill, using the gears to save effort. Most cyclists plug away in too high a gear for far too long and waste energy, so change down early and really use the gears. I shall discuss riding techniques later, but learning to handle the touring machine safely, right at the start, will prove of great benefit to both rider and machine.

First Service

Having bought the machine, equipped it for touring and learned how to ride it, the next step is to go out for a few long, unladen rides. To begin with, restrict yourself to about 20 miles or so, but try to include a variety of terrain. You should be able to average around 10 mph (16 kph) without undue effort over moderate to hilly terrain, but if you have not cycled for some time, or only ride to and from the office, you will find these rides tiring and, until the saddle is broken in, quite painful. However, that is the object of the exercise. These rides will concentrate your mind most wonderfully on the problems and pleasures of cycle touring, and serve to test the machine.

After you have ridden, say, 200 miles, or after a few weeks' riding, take the cycle back to the shop and have them carry out whatever alterations you think are necessary, and give the machine a thorough service, adjusting brakes and gears. The cycle should by now be well run in, and from this point on your cycle touring days can start.

Machine Maintenance

One of the great attractions of cycle touring is the need for self-reliance. To begin with, you must learn to maintain your machine.

Cleaning

During these early rides, get into the habit of cleaning the machine after each one. If you do, the cycle will never get too dirty, and a quick, two-minute wipe down will be all that is necessary. Quite apart from keeping the machine shining, it will deal with the twin enemies of all moving parts, grit and road dust, to which cycles are particularly prone. All the moving parts need to be kept lightly oiled; however, too much oil can be a menace, blending with grit to form an abrasive paste, so oil sparingly and not too often.

Servicing

All cycle tourists must learn to service their own machines. Quite apart from the fact that setting up the machine correctly is part of the pleasure, you cannot rely on a cycle shop being both handy and open if something goes wrong with your machine. A little know-how can save a lot of time and trouble. As a basic minimum you must be able to repair a puncture, adjust the brakes and gears, and replace a broken spoke. These skills are fairly simple and can be learned from books, or picked up from cycling friends. Start with the simple jobs, and the more painstaking tasks will soon become possible.

Punctures

If the tyres (covers) are fairly new and still have a good clear tread, punctures should not occur too often. Most cyclists carry spare tubes, finding it quicker and easier to remove the punctured tube, fit a fresh one, inflate it and ride on, rather than squat in the gutter and find the puncture by the roadside. Remember to check the tyre and remove the cause of the puncture before fitting the new tube, or that too may quickly deflate.

The punctured tube can be repaired later. The hole can usually be found quite easily by examination, listening for escaping air, or immersing the tyre in a bowl of water.

Brake and Gear Cables

Wire cables stretch and will have to be tightened periodically. In practice, the cables only stretch significantly when first fitted, but on any long tour a reduction in braking efficiency is inevitable. Gear changing can also be affected, as the cable fails to act correctly on the changer. In both cases minor adjustments can be made without much difficulty, using the tool called a third hand. Hoist the cycle wheels off the ground, using an inner tube as a sling if necessary, and check all the adjustments carefully before going on.

Spoke Repair

Well-built tyres are vital; broken spokes will be a mercifully rare experience with good tyres, but one which is sure to happen eventually. When a spoke breaks, the wheel usually goes out of true, and the rim will catch on the brake blocks. It may be possible to use the block release and so continue riding for a while, but with the wheel now weakened, further breakages may occur, so it is better to stop at once and replace the spoke.

If the broken spoke is on the front wheel or the nearside hub of the rear wheel, this is no real problem. All you require is a spare spoke and a spoke key. Remove the broken spoke from the nipple, thread the new spoke through the hub, mesh it with the others and insert the head into the nipple, tightening the nipple with the spoke-key. Elementary truing is then possible, using the chain stays as a guide, and once the wheel is turning smoothly, clear of the chain stays and brake blocks, you can continue riding.

Unfortunately, all too often the broken spoke will be on the chain wheel side and to get a new spoke into the hub you will first need to remove the freewheel block. At this point, most cyclists give up and head speedily for the cycle shop. The action of pedalling tightens the block and removing it usually requires a special tool, called a freewheel remover, and a vice. The wheel is removed from the machine, and the freewheel remover fitted to the block and then into a vice, after which a swift, hard pull on the wheel exerts plenty of leverage and the block comes free – perhaps. While many cyclists suggest ingenious vice substitutes involving drain and manhole covers, my advice, in the absence of a cycle shop, is to try any farm, garage or private house. Many of these will have a vice, and once the block is off, the spoke can be easily replaced.

Replacing the spoke is fairly easy, and after a couple of tries most cyclists can replace a spoke in a few minutes, but wheel truing, like wheel building, is an art. As a rule, though, I can replace a spoke and true a wheel well enough to continue, though I usually take the wheel into a cycle shop at the first opportunity and have it properly trued by an experienced mechanic. In every case it is worthwhile having a go first – this is the only way to learn.

One final point: never remove the rear wheel to replace a spoke or mend a puncture, without first setting the chain on a set sprocket. I usually move it to the smallest one. Nothing is worse than replacing the wheel and then forgetting which gear you were in. If you always put the chain on the smallest cog, a lot of fiddling can be avoided.

Tools and Spares
To service and maintain the machine fully, you will need some tools. The complete list might include the following, although only a limited number can actually be carried on a tour, when you will also need space for a few spare parts.
1. Allen keys: 5, 6 and 7 mm.
2. Rear brake and gear cables (to be cut down to fit the front if necessary).
3. Chain rivet extractor.
4. Chainset spanner and extractor.
5. Campagnola T-spanner.
6. Freewheel remover.
7. Grease solvent, in small can.
8. Puncture repair outfit.
9. Spanners, ring-open-ended, 8–9–10–11–12–13–14 mm.
10. Spoke nipple key, plus spare spokes cut to size.
11. Screwdriver to fit machine screw heads.
12. Spare blocks and shoes.
13. Spanners to fit lock ring and bottom bracket cups.
14. Tyre levers.
15. Two spare inner tubes and one cover.
16. Adjustable spanner.

When buying these items, take the cycle along to make sure that the spanners and screwdrivers fit the nuts and screws of your particular machine, for components vary.

With these tools you can give your cycle regular services and carry out quite complicated repairs and maintenance, stripping down the bottom brake, cranks and hubs, cleaning the gears and cogs, and replacing any parts before they become too worn to function effectively. Servicing a cycle is not a difficult task, but it does call for a certain amount of knowledge and a little practical experience.

Those who are already mechanically minded and can see in general how things ought to go can pick up the detailed knowledge required from any of the service manuals listed in the bibliography, which will give more information than I have space for here. Those of a less practical bent should seek the assistance of a more experienced cyclist, or better still, attend a course of practical instruction.

Security

After the cycle, your second purchase must be a good lock. Cycles are stolen all too often, so chain it up whenever you leave it, even if only for a few seconds. The Citadel lock is practically thiefproof, and therefore recommended.

Insurance

Bicycles get damaged as well as stolen, so insure your machine at once, and make a note of the machine number. The police will also mark your machine with a code which identifies it as yours. Insure the machine for its replacement value (a 'new-for-old' policy), by either adding it to your Household Policy, or insuring it with a specialist cycle insurer suggested by a broker, or with the Cyclists' Touring Club, which has a good insurance scheme available to members.

Start Cycle Touring

'Take a piece of paper' (said Uncle Podger) – he always began at the beginning – 'put down on it everything you can possibly require; . . . see that it contains nothing you can possibly do without. Imagine yourself in bed; what have you got on? Very well, put it down. . . . You get up; what do you do? Wash yourself. What do you wash yourself with? Soap; put down soap. . . . Then take your clothes. Begin at your feet; what do you wear on your feet? Boots, shoes, socks; put them down. A corkscrew; put it down. Put down everything, then you don't forget anything.'

The list made, he would go over it carefully, as he always advised, to see that he had forgotten nothing. Then he would go over it again, and strike out everything it was possible to dispense with.

Then he would lose the list.

JEROME K. JEROME 'THREE MEN ON THE BUMMEL'

Good cycle tours – the ones you will enjoy making, and remember fondly afterwards – have to be planned and prepared. It is possible to bound into the saddle on a bright May morning and just pedal off into the sunshine, but sooner rather than later trouble is sure to come your way. Besides, planning a cycle tour is all part of the fun and, as I found with the tours in this book, unless you work out your route, you miss sights and places which you really ought to see.

Planning can be broken down into six broad categories:

1. Clothing and equipment.
2. Maps and guides.
3. Sources of information.
4. Accommodation.
5. Pre-trip preparations.
6. Getting to the start and back.

If you consider all these carefully, and the various problems which will inevitably arise are taken into account, there will be more time free for enjoyment and less to worry about. To plan properly, make a list.

Clothing

When it comes to cycle clothing, my personal views differ somewhat from those of the committed cyclists. While I do possess 'proper' colourful, specially designed cycling clothing, I have managed to go on long tours of a month or more in nothing more specialized than shorts, a tee-shirt and a pair of tennis shoes. Many kinds of sports clothing can be used for cycling, but cycling clothes can be used for nothing else. However, having the 'proper' cycling garments can be useful, particularly in the varied climate of Britain.

Cycling garments are comfortable, warm, designed for the task, and regrettably expensive. Let's consider them, and the alternatives, item by item.

Shoes

Cycling shoes are light and flat-soled. The tops are made from leather, often perforated with small ventilation holes. The sole and instep are stiffened with a steel or wood shank to keep this part of the shoe rigid, while the sole itself often has a plate, or cleat, attached which links to the pedal, holding your foot in the correct position and assisting the pedalling action. This type of shoe was originally designed for racing, and since touring has different requirements, touring shoes tend to be a little different. They have a small heel and unperforated uppers, and no metal cleats which can scar floors and make a terrible noise in the hushed precincts of a church or art gallery – although you can of course cycle in shoes with cleats and take another pair for sightseeing. Good makes of cycling shoes are Madison, Cumbria and Siole.

If you want to avoid buying cycling shoes entirely, you can use a good pair of trainers, provided they fit the toe-clips firmly and can be swiftly removed from them when you come to a stop. As I have already said, if your shoes stick in the toe-clips at this moment you will fall off. On balance, then, most tourists will invest in a pair of touring shoes with a small heel.

Socks and Stockings

Cycling is warm work, and once your legs are moving well, socks or stockings may be unnecessary, but they are certainly welcome outside the warm days of summer, and early in the morning when the air is chilly. In the fringe months of spring and autumn I recommend long stockings.

Shorts

Special cycling shorts are always black, long in the leg, made of close-fitting stretch material, and padded in the seat with either chamois leather or a polyester fabric, which is easier to wash. Wearing cycling shorts for the first time can make you feel a little odd, but they do have definite advantages. They hug your body, reducing wind drag. The seat padding helps to reduce pressure on your groin, while the back grips your shirt and is cut to prevent a wide expanse of spine being bared to the elements when you are in the saddle. I have managed all my summer tours quite adequately in a pair of tennis shorts (remember not to put anything in the side pockets, or your pedalling legs will soon spill the contents out on to the road), but on chillier days my cycling shorts have come in very useful.

Trousers
Cycling trousers, or longs, are not unlike tracksuit trousers and, like them, are designed either to slip on over your shorts or to be worn separately. They are narrow in the leg, fitted with ankle zips for easy removal, and, like the shorts, have some circular chamois padding in the seat. I have found longs very useful, both for cycling and slipping on to visit some church or building where shorts would be unwelcome. The narrow leg is also an advantage, for anything too wide or baggy will probably catch in the chain and will certainly get smeared with oil. A pair of cycling trousers is a worthwhile purchase, though many cyclists prefer breeches and long stockings.

Shirts and Jerseys
Most committed cyclists wear a short-sleeved wool or wool-acrylic mix cycling jersey in bright colours, often those of their local club. The colours should help to alert motorists, and the jersey has pockets at the back of the waist, which can hold maps, money or a snack (pockets at the side or front will soon spill the contents).

Personally, I don't find these cycling jerseys very useful, and prefer to wear a tee-shirt with a pullover added in the morning, or until I warm up. Follow the 'layer' principle – two thin garments will be warmer than one thick one, because of the insulating air trapped between them. I like to have a layer which I can strip off when I start to get hot, and put on if I stop or feel cold.

Jerkins
Cycle jerkins, on the other hand, are very useful indeed. Like the jerseys, they come in bright colours and usually have a woollen back and sleeves, rear pockets, and a wind- and showerproof outer lining in

35

nylon. This is a great help in keeping your body warm when battling against a headwind or sweeping down from a high, cold pass early in the day. A cycle jerkin would certainly be a worthwhile investment.

Many other outdoor garments can be pressed into service for cycling quite effectively, and in various combinations. I have found a fibre-pile jacket very comfortable, and added a sleeveless down ski-jerkin on one cold winter's ride, for a little extra warmth. Choosing the ideal combination of garments is difficult, because once you have warmed up excess garments have to be taken off and stowed in the panniers until needed again, and that can use up valuable space. As a rule, I manage quite well with a tee-shirt, a pullover and a cycling jerkin, and one or more of these caters for most climatic conditions from the chilliest mornings to sun-scorched afternoons.

Neckerchief
One useful extra is a neckerchief to stop cold draughts or raindrops trickling down your neck, and it will also prove fairly efficacious against bees and other intrusive insects.

Hats and Helmets
A hat can be very useful. The head acts as your body's radiator, and in cold weather the bulk of heat loss occurs through the head. Cover your head and you will stay warmer; remove your hat and you will cool down. Cyclists' caps are rather like those worn by schoolboys, with a short brim, and often have an elasticated wool backing which can be tugged down to cover the ears in winter, with lighter cotton models available for summer. A hat is certainly useful, and practically any kind will do, provided it fits snugly enough not to blow off on a downhill run.

Helmets are a matter for debate. British cycle-touring *cognoscenti* generally regard helmets with scorn, and rarely wear them. In other countries they are more common, but as far as I am aware no country yet insists on their use. I suspect they would be more widely worn if they looked less like pudding basins, but, aesthetics apart, they can prevent serious head injuries. A cyclist can move at considerable speed and is very vulnerable in the event of a collision or a fall. No skull is improved by smiting a car or kerbstone at 20 mph, so helmets have to be recommended if only on the grounds of common sense.

Glasses

If you normally wear glasses, consider getting contact lenses, as it is almost impossible to cycle in the rain while wearing glasses. Many cyclists, myself included, wear sunglasses most of the time when it is dry, not just (or even) because of glare, but because they help to keep grit and insects out of my eyes. They should not be too dark, should fit securely, and be kept in a case when not on your nose; I keep mine in a small belt pouch.

Gloves

These are an essential item. You are bound to fall off occasionally, and without gloves your hands are sure to suffer. Most cyclists prefer string-backed fingerless mittens with padded leather palms. These palms may look superfluous but, apart from protecting your hands in a fall, they help to ease nerve pressure points in your own palms – much of the cyclists's weight rests on the hands, and nerves can get pinched. Riding down to Spain without gloves, I damaged the nerves in one hand, losing a lot of the sensitivity in two fingers, and it was months before the feeling came back; so wear gloves.

For cold weather something more robust is required. I wear full-length, fingered cycling gloves with padded leather palms, rainproof uppers and insulation filling. They are very warm and comfortable, and perfect on winter rides.

Underwear

By the end of a day of cycle touring the cyclist will be nicely coated with a fine paste of sweat and road dust, and there is nothing quite as refreshing as a long, hot shower and a change of clothing when the day's riding is over. Since everything has to be carried, I carry three sets of underwear on a one-on, one-off, one-in-the-wash basis, washing one set every night. Pants should be cotton rather than nylon, and if there are seams on the seat they should be as flat as possible. Otherwise, after an hour or so in the saddle, the cyclist feels like a hot-cross bun. In the colder months thermal underwear is useful, for not only does it provide valuable warmth, but it also helps to absorb perspiration and draw it away from the skin. Even in summer thermal underwear is useful, for it weighs very little and is warm and comfortable to sleep in.

Windproofs

In many parts of the world, even in some parts of Europe, summer weather is warm enough and reliable enough to make rainwear unnecessary. In southern France or Spain I have managed well with just a windproof jacket, quite adequate for sudden storms. In Britain, though, it's different, and any sensible cyclist will invest in at least a cape, or better still, a full suit of windproofs.

Traditionally, cyclists have worn leggings, an oilskin cape and a sou'wester, usually in yellow, which is in fact a very practical combination. The snags are that it is heavy, creates condensation from trapped body heat, and offers large amounts of space to be buffeted by wind and the draught from passing lorries.

For these reasons many tourists now buy full suits of rainwear, a cagoule and trouser combination, which gives good protection from the weather and reduces the impact of wind buffets. These suits are usually made from rip-stop nylon, but in recent years committed tourists have been turning increasingly to garments made of Gore-Tex, a semi-porous material full of holes large enough to let out heated body vapour, but small enough to keep out raindrops. In theory, if Gore-Tex works perfectly, you stay both warm and dry. In practice some condensation is inevitable, but Gore-Tex, though expensive, does usefully reduce the amount of condensation-creating damp inside your garments.

Most of these jackets have a hood (hence the name 'cagoule' – which means a hood), but it is better to leave it folded down in the collar and wear a hat, since with the hood up your visibility and hearing are much restricted. Good raingear should have a full-length zip in the jacket, and gussets in the trouser legs so that they can be slipped on and off easily. Some riders prefer seatless leggings or chaps, which minimize condensation. All pockets and zips should have flaps, to eliminate rain and wind penetration, and the neckerchief mentioned earlier will come in very handy to stop raindrops running down your neck.

Spare Clothing

Take at least one complete change of clothing for the evenings, or if you get soaked to the skin. If you select with care and remember the layer principle, you can carry adequate amounts of clothing and, by ringing the changes, stay smart and comfortable both in the evening and in the saddle. A full range of clothing is given in the kit list (Appendix 2).

Equipment

Although clothing requirements are fairly standard for any kind of cycle tour, the amount of equipment carried for eating and sleeping depends very much on the type of accommodation you choose. If you stay in hotels, hostels or bed and breakfast places, you can certainly carry less equipment. On the other hand camping is cheaper, more flexible and possibly more adventurous. Even if you don't want to camp you may find it useful, or at least advisable, to carry a little basic camping equipment such as a stove, plates, cooking and cleaning gear and a sleeping bag, just in case the accommodation you have to settle for is primitive or non-existent.

Tents

As far as cyclists are concerned, carrying a tent poses two problems – weight and bulk – but these are less of a problem than the beginner might suppose because a wide range of lightweight tents is available, many of them ideal for cycle touring. A good lightweight tent need weigh no more than 4 lb (2 kg) complete with flysheet, inner, poles and pegs, and this can be reduced still further if you opt for a single-skin tent, although in Britain a double-skin tent, one with fly and inner, is recommended. If you tour with a friend, or in a party, you can carry a larger, heavier tent and share the weight of the components among you.

Since it always pays to put the tent up first and strike it last, to have shelter available for as long as possible, the tent should be carried on the pannier rack. It therefore helps if the tent is not too long. Inspect your tent carefully before purchase, and see it both pitched and packed.

The Robert Saunders Jet-Packer or the Packit, which I have used on several tours, is to my mind the perfect cycle touring tent, for it weighs little and packs up very small. Other good models are the Field and Trek Pathfinder, the Vango Microweight, and the Saunders Backpacker II.

Sleeping Bags

Even if you don't intend to camp you might consider taking a sleeping bag, which can offer you a comfortable night's sleep on a hostel bunk, in a church porch or on a friend's sofa. The choice of filling is crucial, and lies broadly between down and synthetics. Personally, I'm a down man and swear by my Black's Icelandic. The advantages of down are exactly the ones which are most required by cycle tourists – lightness and packability. The only snag is that if the down gets wet, the feathers mat and lose all insulation, which is why many lightweight campers recommend synthetic fillings such as Hollofil or Dacron for camping in Britain. However, it is fairly easy to keep a down bag dry while cycling – simply wrap it in a plastic bag and place it high in the pannier. Sleeping bags come in two main shapes, the narrow-at-the-foot 'mummy' bag, and the straight-sided type. I prefer the straight-sided ones, but the choice is a personal one and makes no great difference.

If you want to stay in youth hostels you must also carry a sheet sleeping bag or hire one from the warden.

Sleeping Mats

Since a good night's sleep is enjoyable, if not essential, after a day in the saddle, experienced cycle campers use some form of ground insulation. The three main types are the airbed, the close-cell mat and the self-inflating air mat. Airbeds of the lilo variety tend to be too heavy and bulky, although they are very comfortable. Most lightweight campers choose close-cell pads, such as the popular Karrimat; these can be full- or hip-length, weigh very little and roll up tightly. I find the protection they offer rather inadequate, so I use and recommend a compromise, a Therm-a-Rest air mat, which rolls up tightly, self-inflates when an air valve is opened, and gives good insulation on the hardest ground.

Stoves

A stove is always useful on a cycle trip, if only for brewing a cup of tea beside the road. The question of stoves cannot be separated from that of fuel, where the possibilities are petrol, gas, paraffin, methylated spirits and solid fuel. For cycle touring purposes solid fuel, paraffin and meths can be discounted for a variety of reasons, so that the choice lies between petrol and gas. Luckily the range of stoves in both fuels is wide and suitable.

For roadside brews, and heating a simple evening meal, few stoves are more suitable than a Camping Gaz Globetrotter. The stove is light and compact, and the gas cartridges are easily obtainable. I use one of these in summer and it has performed well for years. I carry one spare cartridge in case the one on the stove runs out of puff in mid-meal. I also use a small petrol stove, the SVEA 123, which is very popular with backpackers, produces great heat and works well in all weathers. This burns best on unleaded fuel or 'white' gas, which is hard to obtain in Britain, but it functions quite effectively on 2-star petrol. Either stove can be recommended for cycle touring. On a point of safety, never light or fill a stove, or change a gas cartridge, inside the tent – the risk of a flare-up or fire is just to great. For the same reason, cooking should be done outside the tent, or at worst in the shelter of the porch, but never inside the inner tent.

Give some consideration to cooking pots and utensils, thinking in terms of adaptability: the lid of a pot might also serve as a plate or frying pan, for example. I use a set of aluminium Trangia pots from Sweden. They weigh very little, fit in the panniers easily, and I can stow a number of smaller items, such as a pot grab, a scouring pad and a drying cloth, inside the pots out of the way, which also reduces rattles. One useful extra is a small Trangia kettle, ideal for quick roadside brews.

Water Containers
Cyclists get through a great deal of water. Cycling is hot, thirsty work, and if the day is halfway clement the sun and warm air will quickly draw out moisture from your body, so that most cyclists lap up water with the extravagance of camels at every opportunity. The standard water bottle does not hold enough to meet the full needs of washing and cooking in the evening, so you have to carry either two water bottles or a plastic water container in the panniers which can be filled on the campsite for the evening's brews. I opt for this latter solution. Many experienced tourists have replaced the small cycling bottle with a plastic squash bottle, which fits the carrier and holds much more water. Drink whenever you can, and drink a lot.

Panniers and Other Bags
Anything you take has to be carried, and the only place to put it is in panniers and on the bike. From time to time you will see cyclists cranking along wearing a rucksack, but this should be avoided, if not actually deplored. A cyclist wearing a rucksack is overloaded, off-balance and excessively prone to buffeting, so don't do it.

The full range of specially designed cycling luggage consists of front and rear panniers carried on racks over the front and rear wheels, a saddlebag, and a handlebar bag, which all together, or in various

41

combinations, will cater for any amount of luggage and all types and length of tour. I have seen tourists riding bikes on which every tube had a pannier, but I find a saddlebag and handlebar bag adequate for short hotel or hostel tours, while long cycle camping trips of up to a month can be well enough catered for with two rear panniers and a handlebar bag, provided that certain bulky items, such as tent, sleeping pad and windproofs, can be carried on the top of the pannier rack.

There are many makes of pannier on the market: Carradice, Karrimor, Hague and Packit, to name but a few. Raleigh have panniers specially to fit the racks on their touring machines, but by and large the systems of rack and pannier are interchangeable. When buying a set of panniers, inspect each item thoroughly and examine the seams and fastenings closely, for these are the keys to good workmanship. The best bags are made in grazeproof Cordura fabric, have interior sealing baffles under the main flap, and plenty of small exterior pockets for items you may need during the day, such as tools or maps.

All zips should seal tightly and be flapped against rain and road spray. No material is truly waterproof, so always wrap the contents in plastic bags, and keep the flaps tightly shut against moisture. I use and recommend Karrimor panniers – the Iberian range is a particular favourite. I can get my maximum gear into two rear panniers and a handlebar bag, and so far have never needed to add front panniers or a saddlebag.

Packing the panniers is an art which usually takes a little practice, with two or three false starts each time in an effort to get everything in neatly. After a day or two on tour I can usually pack up and be away in well under thirty minutes. The basic rule is that the heavy items in the rear panniers must, for the sake of balance, be packed as low as possible, and to the front of the bag, towards the centre of the cycle. It is also important to put in last the items which come out first. The simplest way to explain this is to list how I pack each pannier.

Right rear pannier	Stove, food, fuel, sleeping bag (in plastic bag), spare tyre, cookset.
	In small rear pocket: Inner tubes, puncture outfit.
Left rear pannier	Spare clothing (in plastic bag), first aid kit, washing kit, windproofs, spare sweater, gear.
	In small rear pocket: Tools.

On pannier rack	Sleeping mat, tent, poles, pegs (if camping).
Handlebar bag	Maps, notebook, film, camera, wallet, any valuables, cycle lock.

The object is to have the bags shut in the morning, and keep them that way until the evening, unless I need the windproofs or stop for a brew. I carry all the valuables in one place, the handlebar bag, and if I leave the bike, even to look in a shop window a few feet from the kerb, I take the handlebar bag with me and I lock the bike as well. It takes a few seconds, but eternal vigilance is the only way to deter theft.

Having packed the panniers, give them a good shake and try to eliminate any irritating rattles, then compare their weights, moving items about if necessary, trying to spread the load evenly. When you put the panniers on the bike and wheel it up and down the frame will seem to wobble and flex alarmingly at first, but after a few miles you get used to it.

First Aid

Any thoughtful traveller will carry a small first-aid kit, and cyclists are no exception. Blisters may be rare, but grit or an insect in the eye are fairly common, and grazing falls not unknown, so the kit should contain an eye lotion as well as the usual range of salves and plasters. Cyclists are also prone to sun- and windburn, and should apply plenty of sun oil and a lip salve until the skin gets toughened. Remember that sweat will wash the sun oil off quite quickly, so apply a little more at regular intervals.

Maps and Guides

The main part of this book describes twenty cycle tours in Great Britain, but no sensible cyclist rides about reading a guidebook or, while on one tour, weighs the bike down with the details of nineteen others. Cyclists use maps.

Maps

The Cyclists' Touring Club (CTC) recommends the Ordnance Survey (OS) 1:250,000 (4 miles to 1 in.), the Bartholomew 1:100,000 ($\frac{5}{8}$ in. to 1 mile), or the OS 1:50,000 ($1\frac{1}{4}$ in. to 1 mile) for touring. Maps, however, have to be divided into categories – those used for choosing and planning a trip, and those used while riding.

I advise you to use a minimum of 1:250,000 scale for planning, and a 1:100,000 scale for riding, and there are several good reasons for this. It is much easier to plan a tour and avoid missing good roads if the bulk of the route can fit on to one, or at the most two, maps. That means a fairly large scale, but the map should, in addition, show the terrain and the minor roads which you will use whenever possible. The scale should be large but not too large, and 1:250,000 is about right.

On the road you will often wish to wander, and it is much easier to know where you are with a map scaled at 1:100,000 or less. The snag here is that on a long tour many maps may be necessary, and that can be expensive, especially since cycle touring is hard on maps, which do not stand up well to constant folding and unfolding. A full set of 1:50,000 O S maps currently cost over £200, a fairly heavy investment, as much as a good new bike, so something less expensive seems advisable.

My ideal cycle touring maps would be a national series of 1:250,000 maps covering the entire country, each sheet giving details of places of interest, terrain, minor roads and gradients, with distances between even small centres, and *all* the road numbers. Finally, the total set should not be too expensive. After a long afternoon in Britain's largest and most specialized map shop (Stanford's, 12–14 Long Acre, London WC2P 9LP (tel: 01–836 1321)), I could not find a series which matched the criteria completely, and would urge some British map publisher to match the touring maps produced by the Institut Géographique National in France, which are models of their kind. The compromise I settled on was the Bartholomew GT (Grand Touring) series, and all the tours in this book are designed to follow them. The scale is 1:250,000, the series is complete and covers the entire country, Scotland, England, Wales, on ten sheets, and the current (1984) price of the complete set is £17.50. The maps show minor roads and give some indication of terrain, showing spot heights, distances in miles on A and B roads, and give enough detail to enable your route to be plotted with some accuracy. Cyclists who want to plot and plan any of the tours given in this book will need the relevant GT map.

The details which head each tour description in this book, also list the other maps of a smaller scale, including the Bartholomew 1:100,000 scale, which is popular with cyclists. Readers will find no lack of British mapping, in a wide range of scales, in any good bookshop.

Guidebooks

Every good cycle tour should have a theme, and every good theme is improved if you know the story behind it. A list of suggested titles which might be consulted heads each tour description, and the bibliography is even more comprehensive. I do urge you to read them while planning your tour. Since no cyclist can ride about with a library, do your reading up beforehand and transfer the necessary information into a small notebook, which in the months or weeks before the tour will fill up with plenty of useful, if fragmented, information.

Compiling a Notebook

It might help beginners to list some of the sub-headings the notebook might contain. A glance through some of my own reveals the following:
1. A kit list.
2. A timetable for booking tickets, servicing the bike, packing it, and trial rides.
3. A day-by-day route guide, to be marked on the map or maps (often a different route from the one actually covered, but useful all the same).
4. Maps to buy. Books to read.
5. Accommodation, with phone numbers. When to book.
6. Cycle shops en route, gleaned from cycling magazines or the appropriate Yellow Pages (your local library may have these).

The pages of my notebooks are crammed with scribbled notes, snippets of information culled from magazines, books or friends. 'Go west to shelter from prevailing wind', 'Early Closing Day Thursday', 'House shut, but gardens open, Nov. to Apr.'. I write up these notebooks daily on tour and they have provided the basic information for this book.

Daily Stages

The tours in this book assume a daily average of approximately 50 miles (80 km). Please note the word 'average'. The distance you can cover depends on a host of factors: weather, terrain, weight carried, the fitness of the rider and the length of the tour. On an extended tour, over two weeks, any rider will get fitter and cover greater distances each day, but an unfit rider will not cover any great distance with ease in the course of one week. I have selected 50 miles partly on the advice of other cyclists, but mainly because I aim for that myself. It remains an average. I might start with 30 miles a day, and once I get a little fitter, on a good day, with a level road and a following wind, I might reel off 80. It depends.

There is also a considerable difference between the distance planned and the mileage on my milometer – those little side trips to see a church or visit a pub all add up. Don't start off at a great rate, but travel at a speed you can maintain, hour after hour, day after day, without difficulty. It is not supposed to be exhausting.

Consider 10 mph (16 kph) a decent speed, reckon on spending from 9 am to 6 pm on the daily tour, and this should allow for 50 miles (80 km) a day with adequate stops for sightseeing, rest and refreshments.

On a personal note, I don't regard covering vast distances as important. It's how you travel that counts, not how far or how fast.

Gradients

Britain is unfairly endowed with short, steep hills, which demand much effort for the ascent, without the prize of a restful downhill swoop on the far side. A morning cranking over these switchback hills can be wearing. Sensible cyclists, committed to one set of gears, will take a little time each day to study the map and plan a route around these heartbreak hills. There are exceptions to this rule, for some ascents offer glorious views and are worth attempting for the rewards of the summit. I have even heard of cyclists who *like* climbing hills, but I have never met any. Then point is that, when hills lie in your path, they can reduce the daily mileage.

Road Surfaces

Some are as smooth as silk, and you will roll over them gently with minimum effort. Some offer such resistance to the tyres that a loaded cyclist has to pedal hard even when riding downhill! You soon become an expert at riding along the smooth, narrow, painted concrete strip of the verge marker, rather than forcing the cycle over the rough drag of the macadam. There is not much that can be done about road surfaces, which are constantly changing anyway, but again, they do affect your mileage.

Winds

The cyclist is always beating into air resistance, and when the wind is a headwind, life becomes very hard indeed. Experienced riders will set out early in the morning, before the wind gets up, and on a really windy day will wait for the evening, when the wind usually drops. In Britain the prevailing winds are westerlies, blowing in from the Atlantic, so a cyclist riding the End-to-End (Tour 20) should really start at Land's End with the hope of a following wind. Many ride the other way because it is 'downhill' and seems more natural, but punching west across Cornwall can be very hard work, a low-gear ride even for fit cyclists at the end of the tour.

Fitness

This subject will come up frequently. It helps immensely if you are fit enough at the start of the tour to complete an average day's stage without exhaustion. Riding that distance day after day is still a challenge, but this should be the minimum level of fitness to aim for. The only way I know of to get as fit as this is to go cycling, and clearly people who ride to and from work will have an advantage, not least in getting rear end and saddle compatible. Those who are less fortunate should make every effort, in the weeks before the tour, to ride in the evenings and at weekends.

Sources of Information

For basic information on the area you plan to visit, apply to the English, Scottish or Welsh Tourist Boards, and their Regional Boards, whose addresses are in Appendix 3. The British Tourist Authority also maintains offices abroad (Appendix 3) and can assist overseas cyclists contemplating a tour in Britain. Airlines, tour operators' brochures, magazines and books are also useful sources of relevant background information on what to see, where and when to go, accommodation and routes.

For information of particular importance to cyclists contact the Cyclists' Touring Club (for address see Appendix 1), the oldest and largest cycle touring club in the world. The CTC Touring Department is full of information; the Club runs a useful shop, publishes a bi-monthly magazine called *Cycletouring*, and through a spreading network of local clubs and district associations does a great deal to foster cycle touring at home and abroad. All British cycle tourists should join the CTC, and cyclists from overseas will find the CTC unfailingly helpful.

Other useful and relevant organizations are the National Youth Hostels Associations and a number of the more specialized cycling and camping clubs; a full list is given in Appendix 1. A great deal of information can also be culled from the pages and letter columns of the cycling magazines (see bibliography). The basic rule for obtaining information is to specify what you *want* to know, then think of who *needs* to know it, as a source of information. This 'need to know' route can be very helpful if any more obvious source proves inadequate.

Two final points are worth stressing. Information is worse than useless if it is incomplete or inaccurate. It is depressing to ride miles over the hills to visit some particular castle, only to find it closed that day. Use sources as close to the subject as possible, and always check the information personally before accepting it as correct.

Accommodation

Cycle tourists will find a wide choice of accommodation available in Britain, at a very wide range of prices, from luxury hotels, through boarding houses, bed and breakfast establishments, youth hostels and camp sites. The simple rule for all types of accommodation is the same: book ahead. At the end of the day you will crave a hot shower, a change of clothes and a good meal. Don't put these in jeopardy by neglecting to reserve your accommodation.

Hotels
British hotels, even those in the remote countryside, tend to be expensive by international standards. All will welcome cyclists.

Boarding Houses (Guest Houses)
These are a typically British phenomenon, usually found in seaside resorts. They are cheaper than hotels, and usually offer half-board accommodation – dinner, bed and breakfast – at reasonable rates.

Bed and Breakfast
Bed and breakfast has always been the type of accommodation most favoured by cyclists, for B and Bs offer a warm welcome, a secure

place for the bike, a bath or shower, a comfortable bed, and a full English breakfast next morning. They are also cheap. The CTC and the Ramblers' Association produce an annual *Bed and Breakfast Guide*, available from the CTC and certain outdoor activity shops and bookshops, crammed with addresses and much useful information. Every cycle tourist should buy this guide as a basic source of information. Another excellent bed and breakfast guide is *The Best Bed and Breakfast in the World* (see bibliography), which lists some seven hundred excellent B and B establishments in Britain, whose average 1985 price is £7.50 per head per night.

There is a certain degree of overlap between hotels, boarding houses and bed and breakfasts, and they can occupy some very varied accommodation from manor houses, mills, converted barns and farms to semi-detached urban villas or country pubs. It always pays to copy out likely addresses and telephone numbers into your tour notebook, mark the locations on the map, and do phone ahead to book.

Youth Hostels

No longer simple, spartan lodgings for the impoverished young, youth hostels have changed a lot over recent years. They still offer good, comfortable accommodation, often in out-of-the-way districts, and are usually full of like-minded outdoor enthusiasts. Full details on membership can be obtained from the Youth Hostels Association (England and Wales) or the Scottish Youth Hostels Association, whose addresses are given in Appendix 1.

Campsites

Great Britain is not well provided with or well served by campsites. Perhaps it has something to do with the weather, but with some honourable exceptions, British campsites in general fall short of international campsite standards.

The better campsites are usually found in the popular outdoor districts – in the Highlands, the Lakes and the Peak District – rather than in the more urban tourist areas. Apart from organized or official sites, though, Britain has plenty of scope for wild camping, either on farms or in forests, with the permission of the farmer or the Forestry Commission, or out of sight and out of mind on the remoter moors and mountains. There are a large number of campsite guides, and the camping magazines publish regularly updated site reports which are well worth noting.

Getting to the Start

The ideal cycle tour will begin and end at your own front door, but most people enjoy travelling further afield, while tourists coming from abroad are very dependent on public transport if they are to get off on their tour quickly and make the best use of the available time. Next to riding to the start, the best thing is to find some friendly soul who will ferry bikes and riders to the start of the tour by car and pick them up again at the finish. Some people are that lucky! As a general rule, cycles are not carried on buses or on the long-distance coach services, so most of the travelling has to be done by train – and here a problem arises.

Rail Travel

In spite of much talk to the contrary, British Rail does carry cycles on most routes, and the staff are generally helpful. The snag is that the carriage of cycles is always subject to space availability and does not apply to all routes, or indeed to any route all the time, and the situation is constantly changing. British Rail is always producing leaflets setting out the current situation, but they are so crammed with ifs, buts and exceptions as to be useless.

However, all is not lost. Go to the nearest British Rail Information Office and tell the staff what you want to do, for instance 'How can my bike and I get from London to John O' Groats by next Saturday?' A straight question will usually elicit a straight answer, often with helpful alternatives. In practice I have had no difficulty getting my bike to the start of any tour, or home again afterwards. I have sometimes had to start early or finish late, waiting for the right train, but it has always been possible.

Cyclists from overseas should allow an extra day if they want to travel by rail in Britain, to allow for unexpected delays.

Air Travel

This form of travel is easier, for most airlines in Britain carry cycles, within the baggage allowance. It is usually necessary to remove the pedals, turn the handlebars parallel to the top tube, and in some cases remove the front wheel. Provided the tools are handy, this need take no more than a minute or so at the check-in desk. I also now carry an axle bolt which I fix across the front forks to prevent them being crushed. It is sensible to advise the airline that you are taking a bike, (while tandems are welcome, tricycles are not) and arrive a little early at the check-in desk to avoid the crowds.

How to Make the Best Use of This Book

To please Uncle Podger, make a list. A list, if correctly and comprehensively laid out, will provide the backbone of your tour. This book, and the basic advice which heads each tour, will provide the framework on which the structure of the trip can be assembled. Having selected a tour:

1. Mark out the route of the tour on the Bartholomew GT 1:250,000 map.
2. Write to or ring the local tourist authority (or the BTA offices abroad) for whatever information they can provide.
3. Obtain and read the local or regional guidebooks.
4. Consider the broad details, such as when to go, where to stay, composition of the party, etc., early in the planning stage.
5. Having decided on points 1–4, work out the timings leading up to the date of departure.
6. Check out, in detail, how you will get to the start and home again. This, too, has to be done early in the planning stage.

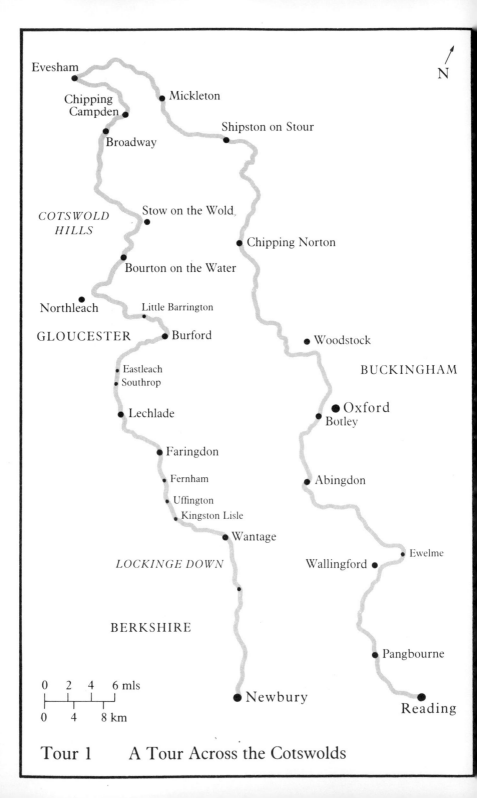

N

Evesham
Mickleton
Chipping Campden
Shipston on Stour
Broadway

COTSWOLD HILLS
Stow on the Wold
Chipping Norton
Bourton on the Water
Northleach
Little Barrington
GLOUCESTER
Burford
Woodstock
Eastleach
Southrop
BUCKINGHAM
Lechlade
Oxford
Botley
Faringdon
Fernham
Abingdon
Uffington
Kingston Lisle
Wantage
Ewelme
LOCKINGE DOWN
Wallingford
BERKSHIRE
Pangbourne
0   2   4   6 mls
0   4   8 km
Newbury
Reading

Tour 1   A Tour Across the Cotswolds

TOUR 1

A Tour Across the Cotswolds

Beauty is Nature's brag, and must be shown.
JOHN MILTON

Distance   237 miles
Time   Five days
Counties   Berkshire, Oxfordshire, Gloucestershire, Worcestershire
Maps   GT Series No.4 (Midlands)
       National Series No.8 (Reading and Salisbury Plain), No.14
       (Oxford)
Guidebooks   *The Cotswolds*, J. Allan Cash (Spurbooks)
         Portrait of the Cotswolds, Edith Brill (Hale)
         A Visitor's Guide to the Cotswolds (Moorland Publishing)
         Red Guide to The Thames and Chilterns (Ward Lock)
Starting points   Newbury, Reading, Evesham

This tour will take the traveller through countryside which many regard as archetypal England, a patchwork of open downs and fields lined with dry-stone walls, through quiet villages and old market towns, across a great variety of landscape, much of it virtually unvisited by the car-borne tourist. For me it is an area rich in memories, since I went to school near Newbury and spent many weekends and my summer holidays exploring this countryside by bike. Returning there thirty years later, it was surprising to find how little it had changed. The lanes are still quiet, the people still friendly, the churches mostly unlocked, the villages unspoiled. The Cotswolds, which you will cross on this journey, are a delightful part of England, but the tour also takes in the windy Berkshire Downs and some little-known places in the Thames Valley.

This is almost a circular tour, and the 17-mile gap between the start at Newbury and the end at Reading is over fairly flat roads and no real obstacle for those who want to complete the loop. As a circular tour it can be joined at almost any point, and Evesham would be a good starting point for cyclists coming from the Midlands or the north.

The distances are not great but the terrain is hilly, especially in the

Cotswolds, but the hills, if steep, are fairly short, offering marvellous views, for example, over the Vale of Evesham, the Vale of the White Horse, or into the deep, secret valleys of the Cotswolds. I made this journey in spring, a late-flowering May, and I can't think of a better time to do it. I see it as a long Bank Holiday trip for the fit cyclist or a one-week introduction for those new to cycle touring. There is a lot to look at, so allow plenty of time for sightseeing. Those who follow this route and stick to the country lanes will have no problems with traffic, even in high summer, and there is plenty of accommodation available, much of it in small country pubs.

The tour begins in Newbury, an historic market town in the valley of the river Kennet and a place worth exploring. It saw two great battles during the Civil War, has a fine museum and some good domestic architecture. The A34 is the artery leading to the north, but pick up the minor road west of this for Donnington (1 mile), a pretty village overlooked by the tall tower of Donnington Castle, all that remains of the medieval fortress which Cromwell besieged and clearly knocked about a bit.

From here our road, the B4494, leads north, under the M4, climbing steadily to the top of the Berkshire Downs at Lockinge (11 miles). Notice here the Ridgeway, the most ancient trackway in Britain, noted on the map as the Icknield Way, and now the route of the 80-mile Ridgeway Path which runs from Avebury to the west, east and north to Ivinghoe in Buckinghamshire. If you are surprised at the width of the Ridgeway here on top of the Downs, remember that it was really a drove road down which sheep and cattle were herded to market, high above the swampy, wooded valley below. From this high point the road drops down to Wantage (3 miles), another small, attractive market town. The Square in Wantage is dominated by a fine statue of Alfred the Great, one of the most famous of English kings. Wantage was his capital, and it is still a rather majestic town, set in the open, rolling downlands, a centre for the local farmers. The Downs are full of racing stables and stud farms, and if you decide to spend the night in Wantage, where there are several hotels, you could take an evening ride over the Downs to Letcombe Basset (4 miles), or even to Lambourn.

From Wantage, follow the B4507 west to Kingston Lisle (5 miles) and Whitehorse Hill. It is a steep climb up to the White Horse itself (2 miles), and up there the outline of the Horse is hard to define, but the views across the Vale below are worth the effort. To see the Horse, ride north to Uffington (4 miles) and then look back, to see it prancing across the face of the Downs as it has done for centuries. Continue north, through Fernham, over the B4508 and into Faringdon (4 miles), and then on to a major road, the A417, to Lechlade (6 miles), a small town on the infant Thames, which rises at Thames Head a few miles to the west. Between the two towns lies Buscot Park, built around 1780, full of eighteenth-century furniture and paintings by the Pre-Raphaelite artist Edward Burne-Jones.

Beyond Lechlade the Cotswolds truly begin, a hilly region certainly, but full of streams and minor rivers and wild flowers, with a number of exquisite little villages built in the golden-grey Cotswold stone. Take the A361 north for about a mile, then turn left on a minor road to Southrop and Eastleach (6 miles), the latter a perfect example of a Cotswold village. In fact two villages make up Eastleach – Eastleach Turville and Eastleach Martin – which are linked across the river Leach by an ancient stone clapper-bridge known as Keble's Bridge after the local lords of the manor, the Kebles, who lived here from the sixteenth century and, incidentally, founded Keble College in Oxford. Eastleach is very photogenic.

Follow the road out, turning east through Westwell into Burford (6 miles), a very fine old Cotswold wool town, whose church of St John was built in the fourteenth century on profits from the wool trade. Cromwell held and tried some of his soldiers here for mutiny and, finding three guilty, had them shot in the churchyard. There is a marvellous wildlife park, and a local history museum in Tolsey House. Burford is a splendid place to stay, well worth a full day's exploration.

On leaving, pick up the small lane which leads west, beside the river Windrush, to Little Barrington, and so on to another pearl of the Cotswolds, Northleach (8 miles). Here the route turns north for Bourton-on-the-Water in Gloucestershire (6 miles), a popular spot for tourists, for the road runs along beside the little river, which is crossed frequently by flat bridges. In May trees hang heavy with blossom above the stream, and there is much to see and do, including an aviary full of exotic birds and a motor museum. There is also a model replica of the village. Don't be put off by all this, for Bourton is a very pretty spot.

The aim of this tour is to discover the finest Cotswold villages, and the next on the list are the curiously named Slaughters and the Swells.

All four are quite beautiful, built in soft Cotswold stone, set in deep green meadows, disturbed only by the tinkle of water. The Slaughters (4 miles) lie just north-west of Bourton and are my favourites, especially Lower Slaughter, which is linked by the river Eye to Upper Slaughter, where there has been no building since the turn of the century, so it remains unspoiled. Lower Slaughter, however, has the advantage of a marvellous main street beside the river, and the Manor Hotel, which has an Elizabethan dovecote in the garden and some good brass in St Mary's church. The route continues through the Swells, Upper and Lower, to Stow-on-the-Wold (4 miles). The very names are irresistible.

Unlike many Cotswold villages, which lie in the valley, Stow occupies a hilltop; it is a place to wander about in, full of old houses. The market square is the site of a twice-yearly fair, held in May and October. The town stocks are still in working order and can be tried for size. Stow would be a good place to stay overnight before picking up the B4077 through Upper Swell and heading west over rising, rolling countryside for 6 miles to where a minor road turns north, near Temple Guiting, for Snowshill, and then sweeps down into the valley and the village of Broadway (6 miles) in Worcestershire.

Broadway is an English gem, very beautiful and therefore rightly popular with tourists. The Lygon Arms Hotel is a mecca for visiting Americans, as is the wide main street, full of antique shops. The road rises, first to the Fish Inn and then up to Broadway Tower, which stands high on the 1,000 ft (330 m) contour. This tower is a folly, built by the Earl of Coventry in 1800 so that he could see his family seat at Worcester, nearly 20 miles to the north-west.

Ride around Broadway, then ride out to Chipping Campden (5 miles), said to be the finest town in the Cotswolds. Chipping Campden was a centre for the Cotswold wool trade, which underpinned the prosperity of medieval England; it is to remind us of this fact that to this very day the Lord Chancellor sits on the Woolsack in the House of Commons. Many of the town's buildings and the church of St James were built with money from wool. St James's contains a memorial to the merchant William Grevel, 'the flower of the wool merchants of all England'. The Woolstaplers' Hall in the High Street dates from the late thirteenth century, when the trade was at its height, and now contains a museum. Chipping Campden is the perfect place to stay and a good touring centre. Do not leave before visiting Hidcote Manor (4 miles), a little to the north, which has magnificent gardens.

ABOVE Horse-trough beside the road near Stow-on-the-Wold.

BELOW The Market Hall, Chipping Campden.

Leaving Chipping Campden on a minor road for Weston-sub-Edge, and crossing the border from Gloucestershire into Worcestershire again, sweep down the B4035 into Evesham (8 miles). The Vale of Evesham is fruit-growing country, glorious in the spring with blossom-filled orchards. Evesham, which stands on one of England's many river Avons, is the site of that thirteenth-century battle where the young Edward I, then Prince of Wales, defeated and killed Simon de Montfort at the end of the Barons War. Abbey Park, beside the river, contains the remains of an old abbey, notably the bell tower.

Evesham marks the turning point of this tour. From here the route turns east and then south, heading a little north on the B4510, and then the B4085, to pick up the minor road to Mickleton – with another chance to see Hidcote – and so to North Littleton on a road which climbs steadily over the crest of the hill to Ebrington and on to the B4035. Follow this east, across the Roman Fosse Way, now the A429, to Shipston-on-Stour (15 miles). Shipston is fairly unremarkable when compared with the places we have seen so far, but good things lie all about it. A few miles away lies Compton Wynyates, a splendid brick-built Tudor mansion, with marvellous topiary in the gardens. Don't miss St Mary's Church in the grounds with its magnificent collection of heraldic emblems, the hatchments of the Comptons. A little to the north lies Edgehill, scene of the first battle in the Civil War.

Turning south now, down to the river Stour at Cherington, ride on to Great Rollright and yet another market town, Chipping Norton (10 miles), a pretty place full of antique shops. Just north of the town lie the megalithic Rollright Stones, a circle of about seventy standing stones, said to represent a king and his army turned to stone by a witch. I say 'about' because it is hard to arrive at an accurate figure, and local legend has it that anyone who can count the Stones and arrive at the same figure three times running will soon die; the risk hardly seems worth it.

Take the A361 and then the B4026 out of Chipping Norton, first for Charlbury, then on to the hamlet of Fawler, where the route turns east for Stonesfield, and then round the western edge of Blenheim Park for the A4095 and into Bladon. Sir Winston Churchill is buried in the churchyard here, and it is only a short ride from here to the home of his ancestors, the Dukes of Marlborough, at Blenheim Palace in the town of Woodstock (13 miles), another good place to stay.

Both the house and park are magnificent and well worth a visit, while Woodstock itself is more ancient and very agreeable. It was once a royal manor, and Edward, the Black Prince, was born here. The Country Museum has a fine collection of farm waggons, and the Bear Hotel opposite is one of the great inns of England.

From Woodstock brave the traffic of the A34 south for about 6 miles to the great roundabout on the Oxford ring road. With a little care you will find the lane to Godstow Nunnery, where Henry II's 'fair Rosamund' was once incarcerated, and the Trout Inn by the Thames. The Trout is a marvellous riverside pub. Look down from the terrace and see the huge trout in the river, have a drink and then, perhaps, ride on into Oxford and take a day or two off to explore the city.

The cyclist's road out must again follow a main road for a while, to Botley, where a minor road runs parallel to the A420, leading to Cumnor, Boars Hill, and down the B4071 into Abingdon, a fine Thames-side town with a magnificent town hall and splendid pubs. From here the A416, a pleasant road not over-burdened with traffic, runs west to Dorchester (8 miles). Dorchester Abbey, now well restored, has some fine effigies, a Tree of Jesse window, and the shrine of St Birinius, who was a missionary to the pagan tribes of the Thames Valley. In Saxon times Dorchester was the cathedral city of the Kingdom of Wessex, and this fine abbey church is worth visiting.

Take the A423 south, past the Wallingford turn, until a little further south, at Benson (3 miles), another minor road turns left, round the edge of the airfield and up to Ewelme, another quiet and beautiful village, full of attractions. Here you will find the oldest village school in England; there are fine almshouses in the cloisters of the church, where the graveyard contains the grave of Jerome K. Jerome, author of *Three Men in a Boat*. The church itself holds the tomb of Alice, Countess of Suffolk, the granddaughter of Geoffrey Chaucer. Church, almshouses and school all date from the mid-fifteenth century, and were built by Alice's husband, the Earl of Suffolk. The church furnishings are splendid: there is a fine carved font lid, much medieval blazonry and a magnificent roof. The village itself glitters with the sheen of watercress beds.

From Ewelme the end of this tour is only a short distance away, but there is more splendid countryside to see as the road descends to Crowmarsh Gifford (3 miles), and then follows the B4009 down to the Thames at Goring (6 miles), where a bridge leads across the river to the splendid village of Streatley. Follow the A329 east on the last lap, a rolling 9-mile run through Pangbourne and at last into Reading and the end of your journey.

TOUR 2

The Pilgrims' Way – Winchester to Canterbury

From every shire's end
Of England, to Canterbury they wend
The holy blissful martyr for to seek.
GEOFFREY CHAUCER, *Prologue to The Canterbury Tales*

Distance   184 miles

Time   Six days

Counties   Hampshire, Surrey, Kent

Maps   GT Series No.2 (South Coast)
National Series No.5 (New Forest), No.6 (Sussex), No.9 (Surrey), No.10 (Kent)

Guidebooks   *The Canterbury Tales*, Geoffrey Chaucer (various editions including Penguin)
The Companion Guide to Kent and Sussex, Keith Spence (Collins)
Portrait of Surrey, B. E. Cracknell (Hale)
The Old Road, Hilaire Belloc (Constable)

Starting point   Winchester

The Pilgrims' Way described in *The Canterbury Tales* ran out of London from the Tabard Inn in Southwark; today it is a busy, unattractive road. The route followed in this tour is the old pilgrim road which ran from Winchester to the shrine of St Thomas à Becket in Canterbury Cathedral, and my route sticks as closely as possible to that followed by those medieval pilgrims, many from overseas, who arrived at Southampton and went to Canterbury via Winchester. This road, like all the pilgrim roads of Europe, takes in some pretty places, for a pilgrimage was often an excuse for a holiday or a chance to see the world. Much of the eastern section of this route is now covered by one of England's long-distance footpaths, the North Downs Way, which also leads to Canterbury. Inevitably a lot has changed in the countryside since the fourteenth century, though less than you might suppose. The countryside is still as green, most of the churches still stand, the people are probably more friendly, and the great cathedral of Canterbury is still a magnificent conclusion.

The best guide to the medieval way in Hilaire Belloc's *The Old Road*, first published in 1904. It gives the distance as 120 miles, but modern obstructions such as motorways and urban sprawl have increased the distance considerably.

This thematic ride is different from a normal cycle tour and will give the traveller something of the feel of those early, more peaceful days of pilgrimage, when the pilgrims set off from the cathedral at Winchester and cantered out, heading for the shrine of St Thomas. The word 'canter' is just one relic which that famous journey to Canterbury has donated to the English language.

There is nothing particularly difficult about this ride; the terrain is gentle, the pubs frequent, and there is no lack of accommodation – on this route, which lies inland, away from the popular south coast, there is no real need to book ahead. This road also gives you a chance to see something of this picturesque area, and those interesting places which lie a little off the route, and which, although they have no connection with the Pilgrims' Way, are still worth seeing.

St Thomas – for those who don't know the story – was a worldly cleric and a most unlikely martyr. A lawyer by training, he became Lord Chancellor to Henry II (1133–89), and the King's closest friend; together they ruled England and made it peaceful and prosperous. Henry's great mistake was to make Thomas Archbishop of Canterbury, thinking that they would then control both church and state. But when Thomas relinquished his Chancellorship, he firmly supported the rights of the Church, and blocked Henry's designs at every turn. Their quarrel became the talking point of medieval Christendom and culminated in Henry's famous outburst: 'Will no one rid me of this turbulent priest?'

On 29 December 1170 four of the King's knights took him at his word, broke into the cathedral, where Thomas was celebrating mass, and slaughtered the archbishop on the steps of the chancel, a crime which shook the Christian world and nearly cost Henry his throne. Within a few months miracles were recorded and Thomas was in due course made a saint. The practice of making pilgrimages to his shrine lasted until the Reformation, when Henry VIII's commissioners dissolved the monastery and removed thirty waggon-loads of accumulated treasure. The bones of the saint who had defied an earlier

Henry were dug up and burned, so there is no shrine there today, but the cathedral church of Canterbury remains the mother house of the Anglican Church and is a fitting focus for this journey.

You start in the precincts of Winchester Cathedral, on the green lawn outside the west door to be exact, where cycles can be chained up and safely left while you visit the great church itself, and the town which lies about it. Try and spare at least half a day for this historic place. Personally, I would recommend a day around the sights, evensong in the cathedral and an early start next day.

Winchester was the capital of Wessex and then of England in the time of the Saxons. Later William the Conqueror, who was crowned at Winchester as well as at Westminster, built a castle here, and Henry III, who was born in the castle, built the Great Hall. In the Hall today there hangs a table, said to be the Round Table of King Arthur and his Knights, though it actually dates from the mid fourteenth century and was probably made for Edward III at the founding of his Order of the Garter, the oldest surviving order of chivalry in Europe.

The cathedral was the shrine of St Swithin, who is said to control the summer rains, and has the longest nave in Europe at 556 ft. Many of the old Saxon kings lie buried here, as does the Conqueror's son William Rufus, killed while hunting in the New Forest. Mary Tudor

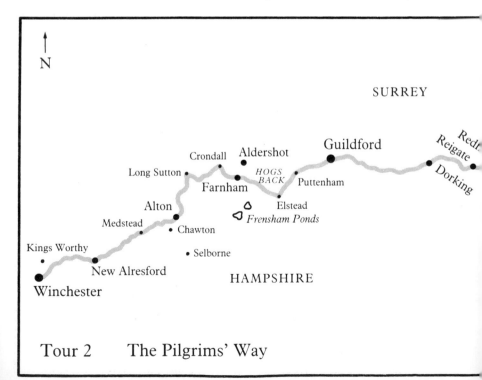

Tour 2   The Pilgrims' Way

married Philip of Spain here in 1554, and the whole building is crammed with history, quite apart from being one of the finest Gothic cathedrals in England.

Across the wide lawns lie the buildings of Winchester College, founded by William of Wykeham in 1394, mainly to provide students for his New College at Oxford. Apart from the school, there is a house once owned by Jane Austen, and much fine architecture.

On the outskirts of the town, on the main A33, lies the Hospital of St Cross, founded in 1136 by Henry of Blois for the shelter of pilgrims. Each day pilgrims who arrive early at St Cross can still receive a dole of bread for their journey. St Thomas' Day is 4 June – the day when his relics were translated to his shrine, not the day of his martyrdom – and in early June this journey is delightful.

Leave by the A33 for the north, which is not as busy as it was before the M3 opened, so with an early start, the road up to Kings Worthy (3 miles) should be fairly peaceful. Here a minor road, and the Pilgrims' Way, turns off for Martyr Worthy and Itchen Abbas (3 miles). The churches at Kings Worthy and Martyr Worthy are both worth visiting but not always open. Vandalism has led to the locking of many churches, even in the countryside, but it is usually possible to obtain the key and, luckily in my case, I arrived on a Sunday.

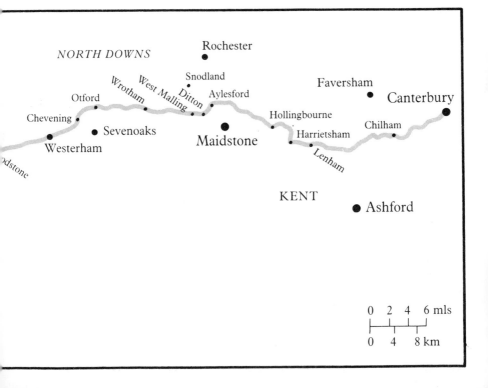

The road follows the river Itchen for a while and then turns towards Northington, but you should carry on along the B3047 for New Alresford (3 miles), on the A31. The country hereabouts is rolling, wooded and very beautiful, and the town is pleasantly set among smooth slopes and copse-dotted hills. From New Alresford a minor road goes north-east, parallel to the A31, running peacefully across country to Medstead and into Alton (10 miles), keeping more or less on the path of the Pilgrims' Way.

Alton is a pleasant market town, a good place for a first stop after a late start, and one evening diversion would be to ride a few miles south down the B3006 to the village of Selborne, home of Gilbert White the eighteenth-century naturalist. Just off the road to Selborne lies Chawton, where Jane Austen lived while writing *Emma*, and the two make a round trip of some 12 miles from Alton.

At Holybourne, on the eastern outskirts of Alton, the route turns north on a minor road, curving round to Lower Froyle, then picking its way across country on minor unnumbered lanes, to Long Sutton and Crondall, all taken with the object of avoiding the A31. After 14 miles you will arrive at the attractive town of Farnham.

Farnham marks a major junction on the Pilgrims' Way, for here those travelling from Winchester met pilgrims from Bristol and the West Country. The town is guarded to the north by its twelfth-century castle, once the principal residence of the Bishops of Winchester. Farnham Castle was besieged, taken and retaken several times during the Civil War, and only ruins remain. There are plenty of good pubs, many of them former coaching inns.

If you decide to stay the night in Farnham you can ride up to Aldershot, the home of the British Army, though I don't recommend it, or ride south a little to the gorse and sandy landscapes around Frensham Ponds, which are worth seeing, before leaving again, heading down the B3001 for Elstead (4 miles). This route runs past the ruins of Waverley Abbey, once a staging post for pilgrims. Then you must pick a way on minor roads to Puttenham (5 miles) and out briefly near Seale on to the A31 at the Hog's Back, a long ridge that drops you down into the county town of Guildford (8 miles), and offers far-reaching views over Surrey on the way.

Guildford has plenty of fine old inns down either side of the steep High Street, a medieval castle which was once the county jail, and

Winchester Cathedral

many bookshops. The town stands on the southern slopes of the North Downs, and the Pilgrims' Way follows the foot of these Downs east along the A25. This is a wide and fairly safe main road, with the Downs looming high to the left and a host of pretty villages on either hand. It passes the springs of the Silent Pool, a rather eerie spot, and so through Dorking (10 miles), Reigate and Redhill (8 miles) to Godstone (5 miles). This 23-mile journey from Guildford to Godstone should take no longer than a short morning, and a further 6 miles brings you to Westerham, a good place in which to break this journey and do a little local sightseeing. Westerham was the birthplace of General Wolfe, who captured Quebec in the Seven Years' War. His statue stands on the Green, while his French adversary, General Montcalm, is commemorated in the name of an hotel.

Breaking from the Way, a good ride to the south would visit such historic houses as Penshurst; Hever Castle, once home of the Boleyns; and Knole, then circling as far as the spa of Tunbridge Wells, before returning to the Way at Chevening, which lies north and a little east of Westerham. From here the B2211 spares you the A25 and from Otford (2 miles) the Pilgrims' Way, now marked as such on the map, leads on to Wrotham (5 miles). Here the A227 leads north, still following the Way, before a minor road takes it east to the river Medway at Snodland (6 miles), where you turn north into the town of Rochester (6 miles), which has a cathedral and a very fine early Norman Castle.

After seeing Rochester, return south to West Malling (8 miles), follow the A20 briefly through Ditton and turn north over the M20. Pass through Aylesford and then turn east at the Bell Inn (2 miles), and again continue down the Pilgrims' Way to Hollingborne (6 miles). This bit of the route is historically accurate and an outstandingly beautiful ride, crossing and recrossing the North Downs which are turning across the Way here, to head south across Kent.

From Hollingborne, follow minor roads and lanes north and east to Harrietsham and Lenham (8 miles), then on to the B2077. Follow this road east to Chilham (15 miles), which has a castle with a Norman keep, and a Jacobean mansion containing a Battle of Britain Museum and a unique collection of birds of prey. Falcons and eagles are kept in the park and display their hawking skills to visitors. The pilgrimage to

Pilgrim Bridge at Aylesford
on the road to Canterbury.

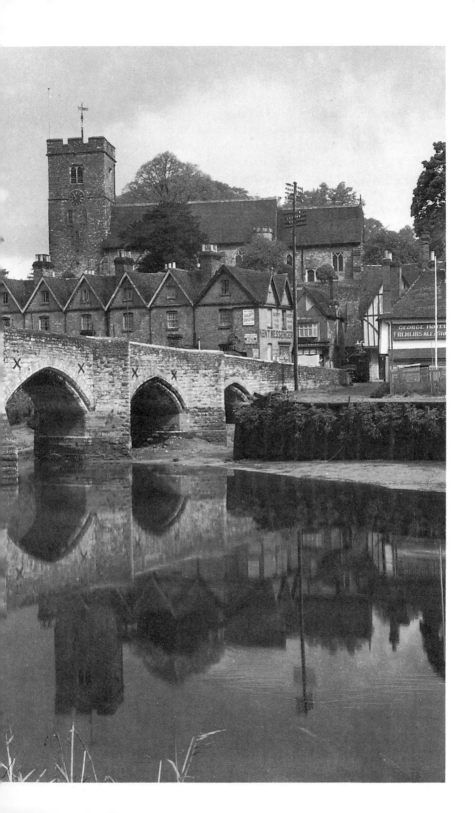

Canterbury also is recalled by the Whitsun Pilgrims' Fair, when the villagers dress in medieval costume and sell goods and flowers in the Square. The Woolpack Inn has seen many pilgrims down the centuries, and is a good place for modern pilgrims too.

The final 6 miles to Canterbury follow the A28 over the last hills and down through the walls and into the old streets of the cathedral city. Like Winchester, Canterbury is well worth giving an extra day to explore the town and visit the cathedral and its precincts, which includes the tomb of Edward, the Black Prince, buried here in 1376. There is also a magnificent fourteenth-century chapter house, and the famous Bell Harry Tower.

Canterbury.

TOUR 3

A Tour of Northumbria and the Border

Walk there awhile, before the day is done,
Beneath the banner and the battered casque.
MURIEL STUART, 'The Tower of Memory'

Distance   311 miles

Time   Two weeks

Counties/Regions   Northumberland, Borders, Cumbria, Durham

Maps   GT Series No.8 (South East Scotland)
National Series No.42 (Northumberland), No.39 (Tyneside and Durham), No.41 (Borders)

Guidebooks   *The Steel Bonnets*, George MacDonald Fraser (Pan)
A View of Northumbria, Geoffrey N. Wright (Hale)
The Scottish Borders and Northumberland, John Talbot-White (Eyre Methuen)

Starting point   Newcastle upon Tyne

This is a tour to the warlike north, the perfect journey for those who love history and travelling in an empty, little-known land. According to the local tourist board, Northumbria is 'Britain's best-kept secret'. It has almost everything the traveller could wish for – empty roads, marvellous scenery, unique towns and quiet villages, a wealth of history and surprisingly mild weather. Best of all, it does seem to be overlooked and underestimated. I met very few other tourists on my travels, which for a region with so much to offer is really surprising. Allow two weeks for this journey for there is a great deal to see.

Before you start on your travels, a note on the name 'Northumbria'. An ancient kingdom, it has not existed since the days of the Saxons, but the name has been revived by the tourist board to cover Durham, Northumberland and Tyne and Wear, and our tour makes a sweep through all three as well as crossing the northern frontier into the Border country of Scotland. (Scotland, by the way, is nowadays divided into regions rather than counties.)

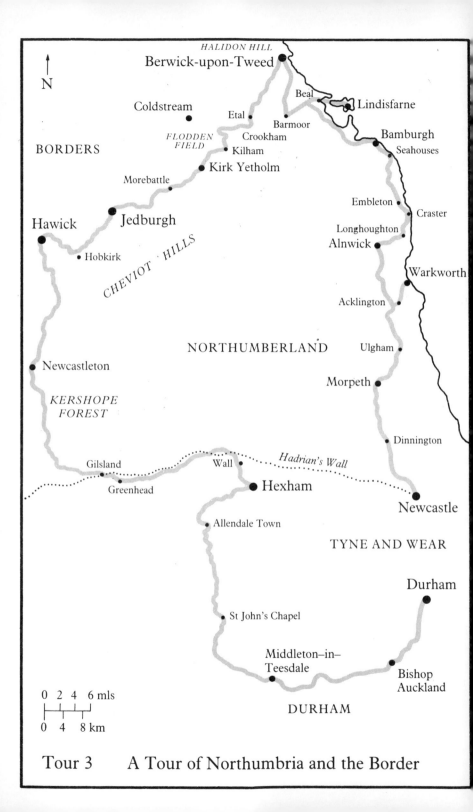

Tour 3   A Tour of Northumbria and the Border

This is a marvellous tour, taking in some splendid places and well worth a full two weeks. The Cheviot and Pennine hills seem to shield Northumbria from the wetter weather, and the only real snag is the easterly winds which can be chilling and relentless, blowing in for days across the North Sea. The terrain is mixed, but not as hilly as you might suppose. I have picked a route that follows rivers or valleys whenever possible, but a few stiff ascents must be anticipated. The journey begins in Newcastle-on-Tyne, which can be easily reached by air, or on the direct rail line from London, and finishes in the cathedral city of Durham.

Newcastle is a busy industrial town where it is all too easy to get lost. If you come by train find the A696 and follow it out of the city towards the airport (5 miles), turning off on the minor road which runs due north for Dinnington and Morpeth (14 miles), a winding ride over fairly flat country and across the river Blythe. Morpeth lies on the A1, the busy Great North Road, so skirt it and pick up the A197 to the east, turning off after 2 miles on to the B1337 which leads across the river Lyne and on to the B6345. This road, too, is fairly gentle and follows the railway line north. Go under the bridge at Acklington (12 miles), on to the A1068, a fairly minor main road, and so into Warkworth (4 miles).

Northumberland is a border county, the scene of frequent fighting over the centuries, and full of splendid castles. Much of Warkworth Castle dates from the twelfth century, and Shakespeare set some of the scenes of *Henry IV* here, in the home of Harry Hotspur. The Grey Mare's Tower has crossbow loops, and the keep looks out towards the sea and Conquet Island, a mile offshore.

Return to the B6345 and follow it into Alnwick, pronounced 'Annick', (10 miles), a fine old town full of narrow streets with medieval names – Bondgate, Narrowgate, Baliffgate, and so on. The Dirty Bottles is the best pub and there are some interesting tombs in St Michael's, the parish church, while many buildings display the stiff-tailed lion of the Percys. Alnwick Castle has been the home of the Percy family since 1309, and much of it can be visited. There are splendid paintings in the Great Hall, an armoury, a coach house and the regimental museum of the Northumberland Fusiliers. The best view of the castle is obtained from the bridge across the water meadows by the river Aln, just north of the town. Half a day here is enjoyable, and it would make a perfect first-night stop.

The Old Priory at Lindisfarne viewed from the harbour.

Leave Alnwick on the B1340, then head for the coast at Long-houghton (3 miles) to pick up the coastal road for the fishing port of Craster (4 miles), famous for kippers. Leave your bike here and walk a mile north along the coast to the ruins of yet another fortress, Dunstanburgh, an eerie place when seen in the morning mist. The sea pounds against the walls, and the Great Hall is said to be haunted. This castle changed hands five times during the Wars of the Roses, and then declined into its present ruined state, but the sight is magnificent and not to be missed.

Continue north, keeping as close to the coast as possible, to Seahouses. From here, if the weather is reasonable and the tides permit, you can go out by boat to the bird sanctuaries on the Farne Islands, a flat and rocky outcrop of rock just visible out to sea.

If this is not possible ride on to yet another castle, still intact and inhabited, Bamburgh (14 miles). From the walls you can see as far as Berwick on the border, 20 miles to the north, while 7 miles away, just across the sea, lies Lindisfarne, which is, for me anyway, the high spot of this tour.

Bamburgh is well worth half a day because there is a lot to see. The Romans built a fort here, and after their legions left it was the seat of the Kings of Northumbria, and then a border fortress which saw frequent fighting during the Anglo-Scottish wars.

Below the castle walls, in the little village church, the heroine Grace Darling lies buried, the girl who rowed herself into history one dark and stormy night rescuing sailors from a ship wrecked on the Longstone rocks. From Bamburgh ride round Budle Bay up to the A1, and then north for 10 miles before turning off right for Beal and Lindisfarne, Holy Island (5 miles). Lindisfarne can only be visited when the tides permit. Don't attempt to cross the causeway if you have been warned not to, for the tide comes in very quickly. There is a small hut perched on stilts in the middle of the causeway to help people who get trapped by the tide.

Lindisfarne has so much to see that a full day is necessary, and as you will have covered nearly 40 miles from Alnwick my advice is to stay the night. There is plenty of accommodation. Lindisfarne is a holy place, site of a community of Celtic monks sent from Iona to preach the gospel to the heathens of Northumbria. The two great saints of Lindisfarne were St Aidan and St Cuthbert, and although their abbey was destroyed by the Vikings the ruins of the later Benedictine abbey, abandoned at the Reformation, still stand. The fine church nearby contains replicas of the Lindisfarne Gospels, while the whole island is overlooked by Lindisfarne Castle, perched on a high spur of dolerite rock on the seaward side of the harbour. The castle was restored by Lutyens at the turn of the present century, and the views from the battery are quite superb. Do not leave before visiting the castle's walled garden, designed by Lutyens' great collaborator, Gertrude Jekyll. Apart from these historic attractions Lindisfarne is a great place for birdwatching, and if you are lucky you may see seals frolicking in the waves offshore as you stroll along the empty, sandy beach.

To avoid most of the busy A1, ride instead on the B6353 to Barmoor (9 miles) and follow the B6525 north, past another castle, following the route of a Roman road to Berwick-upon-Tweed (9 miles). Berwick looks and feels like a Scottish town, and the frontier is not far away. The city walls, which are still intact, were erected on the orders of Elizabeth I, and the barracks, the regimental depot of the King's Own Scottish Borderers, are said to be the oldest in Britain. Berwick offers plenty of good architecture and has a busy harbour. If you like visiting battlefields ride a little to the north, climbing up the A6105 to Halidon Hill where, in 1333, the English archers displayed their prowess by decimating a Scots army.

Leave for the Cheviots by the B6354, which starts with a climb and runs up and down to the village of Etal (9 miles) on the river Till, a green and lovely place. From here it is only a short ride to the battlefield of Flodden (4 miles), where in 1513 an English army, under the Earl of Surrey, defeated an invading Scottish force under King James IV, who was killed in the battle. Many of the dead were buried in the nearby church, which sells a good leaflet on the encounter. It is a muddy spot, and the climb up to the English line on Branxton Hill is very steep. Still on the subject of military history, across the border is Coldstream (5 miles), from where in 1660 General Monck marched his regiment, later the Coldstream Guards, south to London and restored Charles II to the throne. There is a regimental museum in Market Square.

From Flodden Field follow the B6352 to Kilham and then over the border into Kirk Yetholm (8 miles), a typical grim Border town and the end of the 250-mile-long Pennine Way footpath. This area, with the round Cheviots looming up to the south, is known as the

High Force, one of the natural wonders of the North.

'Debatable Land', a battleground for the border reivers, the Steel Bonnets, who, Scots and English, kept the countryside in turmoil for generations until the English and Scottish thrones were united under James I in 1603.

Follow the B6401 into Scotland, through the aptly named village of Morebattle, and into the town of Jedburgh (15 miles), a great centre for the reivers. Jedburgh Abbey, in today's High Street, was constantly being pillaged, and the scorch marks from the various burnings can still be seen on the walls. Queen Mary's House nearby commemorates Mary, Queen of Scots, who stayed here briefly while recovering from a fever, but it was built by the warlike Ker family. The men were all left-handed and so the main staircase spirals left, the better way for left-handed swordsmen to defend their home. Avoid the main road and press on to the next Border fortress, Hawick (12 miles), by the B6357, through Hobkirk to the south. Hawick is a mill town today but it recalls less peaceful times in the Common Riding festivals, held each June. If you want to learn more about the Border wars visit the museum at Wilton Lodge Park on the outskirts of the town.

Up to now the route has skipped swiftly from town to village, but from Hawick it runs south into the wild, empty, rolling country of Liddisdale down the B6399 to Newcastletown (20 miles). This is a fairly hard up-and-down ride, rising to over 3000 ft at one point, but the scenery is splendid. At Newcastletown turn left on to a minor road just south of the town and follow it across the border again into Kershape Forest, on to the B6318, and then south to meet the Roman wall at Greenhead (21 miles).

Hadrian's Wall, which is 72 miles long and runs west from Newcastle to Bowness on the Solway, was built by order of the Emperor Hadrian. Work started in AD 128. It was manned by legionary troops and garrisoned until the end of the fourth century. Considering how long ago that was, much of the Wall is still in a magnificent state of preservation and can be easily seen by following the B6318 east from Greenhead to the village of Wall on the river Tyne (19 miles). The Wall lies just north of this rolling road, set along the crest of the ridge. Housesteads Fort, near Haltwhistle, has been excavated, and the museum there, as well as the one at Vindolanda, should certainly be visited. A half day's walk along the Wall from Housesteads is another enjoyable excursion.

Stay at Wall on the west bank of the Tyne, and then follow the

B6351 down to Hexham (5 miles) before picking up the B6305 for Allendale Town in the open, breezy country to the south. From here it is a steep but lovely ride up Allendale beside the tumbling river to Allenheads and St John's Chapel (20 miles) and, after a brief run east on the A689, across Langdon Common to Middleton-in-Teesdale (12 miles). Then follow the B6282 to Bishops Auckland (23 miles). Charles I was imprisoned in the castle here, and there is a lot of good architecture in this pleasant little town, but the glory of these parts is the cathedral city of Durham (12 miles).

Everything about Durham is splendid: the site itself, with the cathedral rising up above the river Wear, the medieval castle, and the old, leaning houses. At the end of this ride allow at least a day to explore Durham. The Great Hall of the castle is full of armour, while the cathedral is one of the finest Norman churches in Europe. Note the rare sanctuary knocker on the north door which, if he could grasp it, gave freedom to the fleeing criminal. In the museum you can see the remains of the coffin in which the monks of Lindisfarne carried the body of St Cuthbert. The whole city is a mine of history, the perfect place to round off this tour of the wild north of England.

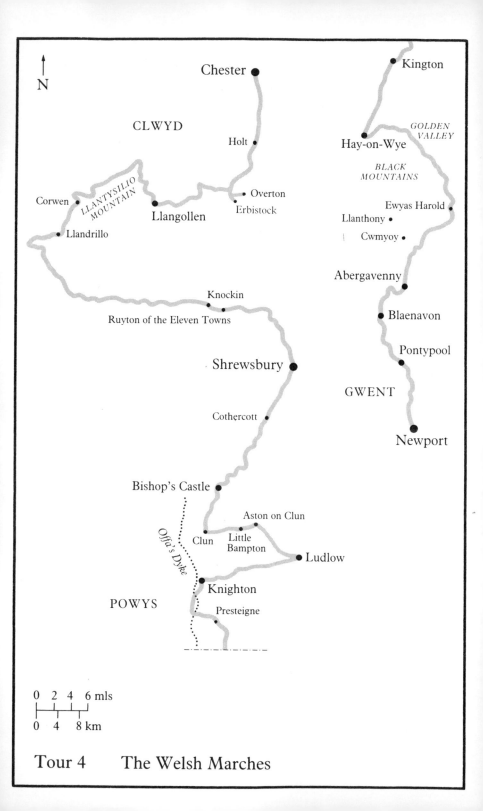

N

CLWYD

Chester

Kington

Holt

GOLDEN
VALLEY

Hay-on-Wye

BLACK
MOUNTAINS

Corwen *LLANTYSILIO*
MOUNTAIN

Overton

Llandrillo Llangollen Erbistock

Ewyas Harold

Llanthony •

Cwmyoy •

Abergavenny

Knockin

Blaenavon

Ruyton of the Eleven Towns

Pontypool

Shrewsbury

GWENT

Cothercott

Newport

Bishop's Castle

Offa's Dyke

Aston on Clun

Clun Little
Bampton Ludlow

Knighton

POWYS Presteigne

0 2 4 6 mls

0 4 8 km

Tour 4 The Welsh Marches

TOUR 4

The Welsh Marches

What are those blue remembered hills,
What spires, what farms are those?
A. E. HOUSMAN, *A Shropshire Lad*

Distance   306 miles
Time   Two weeks
Counties   Clwyd, Shropshire, Hereford and Worcester, Powys,
      Gwent
Maps   GT No.3 (Wales), No.4 (Midlands)
      National Series No.28 (Manchester and Merseyside), No.23
      (Stoke on Trent and Salop), No.18 (Vale of Severn and
      Radnor), No.13 (Hereford and Gloucester)
Guidebooks   *Portrait of the Brecon Beacons*, E. J. Jason (Hale)
      A Visitor's Guide to the Welsh Borders, Lawrence Garner
      (Moorland Publishing)
Starting point   Chester

Having described three tours in England, with a brief foray over the
border into Scotland, it seems only fair to visit Wales and make a ride
which will also present the cyclist with a challenge. This trip, north to
south down the Welsh Marches, covers some splendid country where
the scenery, if rarely flat, is always beautiful. While following a fairly
direct route to the south, the ride also allows for a number of
diversions, so if you enjoy the challenge of cresting steep hills you will
have plenty of chances to do so. The Welsh Marches today reflect
their warlike history, with castles beetling down from the hilltops,
and small, compact villages hidden in the green valleys.

Chester, the start of the tour, can easily be reached by train, and is one
of those cities which you should take a day to explore before riding
out. It has a fine cathedral and dates back to Roman times, when it was
a base for the XX Legion; Roman ruins are plentiful and well
displayed in the museum. Chester's unique feature, though, is the
famous Rows, galleries of shops on two levels which run along several

streets inside the walls which shield the town centre and still encircle the city. Allow a full day for Chester before setting out for the south.

Ride out on the B5130 which runs due south to Holt (7 miles), a fairly easy ride to start the tour. This minor road skirts Wrexham, but American visitors might like to visit the church of St Giles in the town centre, which has not only a splendid tower but also a churchyard with the grave of Elijah Yale, who founded Yale University.

The B5130 encircles the town and meets the A483 (12 miles), where you should turn left, diverting down the A539 for two miles to visit two beautiful villages, Erbistock and Overton, before returning west and following the A539 back into the Vale of Llangollen and down to the river Dee. Llangollen is famous for the annual music festival or Eisteddfod, which attracts singers and musicians from all over the world, but for most of the year it's a quiet place. It has a few unusual features, such as Elseg's Pillar, a standing stone more than a thousand years old, and on the hill to the north the ruin of Castell Dinas Bran, a fortification which dates back to Celtic times. Head north, on the A542, for a stiff 8-mile ride over the Horseshoe Pass (1299 ft). This route takes you past Valle Crucis Abbey, a Cistercian foundation founded by a Welsh prince in 1201 and destroyed by Henry VIII at the Reformation. The abbey church remains, and has a fine rose window and some ancient tombs.

On reaching the A5104, turn left and follow the road to Corwen (8 miles), encircling the bulk of Llantysilio mountain (1804 ft). At Corwen pick up the B4401, and follow it through the Vale of Edeyrnion, past Llandrillo (5 miles) and on to the B4391 (5 miles), where you should turn east for a long and marvellous ride across the Marches to Shrewsbury. This road passes through Knockin on the B4396 (33 miles), a small village south of Oswestry, an attractive place with some early medieval fortifications. Part of the old walls were dismantled to make the two stone bridges at the bottom of the High Street. Top Farm is a splendid black and white house, and the road out leads down a fine avenue of trees past Knockin Hall, a seat of the Earls of Bradford. A mile past Knockin the road forks left on to the B4397 and into the curiously named Ruyton of the Eleven Towns, running along a bluff above the river Perry. The name harks back to 1308, when little Ruyton combined with ten other hamlets in a bid to

opposite A view of Denbigh Moors, Clwyd.
overleaf The ruins of Llanthony Priory.

become a borough. The church is Norman and the churchyard contains the ruins of the Earl of Arundel's castle, built in 1301 and destroyed by the Welsh. Then continue to Shrewsbury on the Severn, which you will reach after a long day's run across some splendid countryside.

Shrewsbury is a medieval town full of leaning buildings and narrow alleyways, with some graceful churches and a much restored Norman castle. Like Chester it is worth a full day's stay. It saw a lot of strife during the Welsh wars, including the execution of David, the last Welsh Prince of Wales, in 1282, and the Battle of Shrewsbury in 1404, when the young Henry V, then Prince of Wales, defeated Harry Hotspur.

South of Shrewsbury a minor road runs down through marvellous country to Bishop's Castle, passing between the rolling mass of the Long Mynd to the east and the more rugged Stiperstones to the west, a ghostly spot as the sun goes down over the hill.

Pass through Bishop's Castle (22 miles), but be sure to stop at Clun, 8 miles to the south, one of those places immortalized in Housman's *A Shropshire Lad*. An old local saying runs:

> Clunton and Clunbury
> Clungunford and Clun
> Are the quietest places
> Under the sun . . .

It wasn't always so. Caractacus, the Ancient British chieftain, made his last stand here against the Romans; the Norman castle whose ruins now overlook the village was besieged constantly by the Welsh; and the church was damaged in the Civil War. Clun is a pretty place to stay in for a day or so, riding out unladen to see the sights round about.

You leave Clun on the B4368, which runs east to Little Bampton, then past Clunbury and on towards Craven Arms. Turn south at Aston on Clun (10 miles) to look at Stokesay Castle, 3 miles to the south, a fine example of a thirteenth-century castle with a moat, gatehouse and well-preserved rooms. From here follow the A49 into Ludlow (8 miles).

Ludlow is a good half-day stop, and since John Betjeman called it 'the loveliest town in England' you may wish to stay longer. Three rivers surround the site and in the past provided the first line in the town's fortifications, which include a Norman castle. The town itself is largely Tudor and Jacobean, with the Feathers Hotel as a perfect example of the architecture of the Tudors, but the whole town is very photogenic, a place to wander in, especially in the evening when long shadows fall across the streets.

Leave Ludlow on the B4361 which heads south, but turn right on to a minor road just outside the town, heading south-west to Knighton (18 miles), a pleasant town standing astride Offa's Dyke, that ancient earthwork built by an eighth-century King of Mercia in an attempt to keep out the marauding Welsh.

From Knighton take the B4357 south to Presteigne and Kington (14 miles), over the hills and eventually on to the B4350 for the town of Hay-on-Wye (12 miles), another frontier town which has become the secondhand book capital of the world. There are bookshops everywhere, and since they will parcel up your purchases and send them anywhere, a day's browsing here would be worthwhile.

South of Hay lie the Black Mountains, a menacing range of hills when the weather turns foul, but marvellous for walking in the milder months of summer. A number of roads run across the mountains, and one popular route, the B4423, goes under Hay Bluff, where the hang gliders hover, and down the Afon Honddu to the ruined priory at Llanthony and the curious church at Cwmyoy, which has suffered from subsidence and, although well buttressed, hasn't got a straight wall anywhere. And so to Abergavenny: this road is a great ride, but very narrow and in summer often jammed with cars. I also had four punctures in as many miles from thorns in the hedge clippings, so if the roads are busy this route is best avoided. I found a better one in the B4348 further east, which runs down the beautiful Golden Valley to Ewyas Harold (20 miles), from which minor roads will take you south to Abergavenny, Blaenavon, Pontypool and the end of this journey at Newport (26 miles).

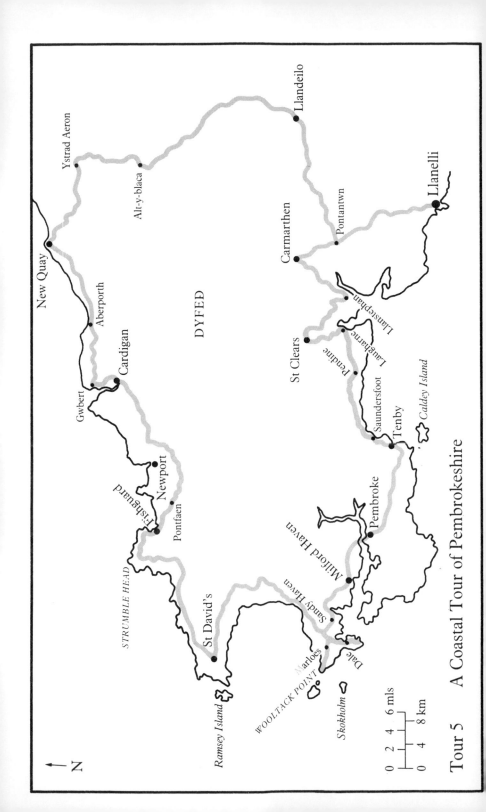

← N

New Quay

Ystrad Aeron

Alt-y-blaca

Aberporth

Gwbert

Cardigan

DYFED

Newport

Pontfaen

Fishguard

STRUMBLE HEAD

St David's

Ramsey Island

Sandy Haven

Marloes

WOOLTACK POINT

Skokholm

Dale

Milford Haven

Pembroke

Saundersfoot

Tenby

Pendine

Laugharne

Llanstephan

St Clears

Carmarthen

Pontantwn

Llandeilo

Llanelli

Caldey Island

| 0 | 2 | 4 | 6 mls |
| 0 | 4 | 8 km | |

Tour 5   A Coastal Tour of Pembrokeshire

TOUR 5

A Coastal Tour of Pembrokeshire

Pembroke is the little England beyond Wales.
THOMAS FULLER, *A History of the Worthies of England*

Distance   262 miles

Time   One week

County   Dyfed

Maps   GT No.3 (Wales)
National Series No.11 (Pembroke and Carmarthen)

Guidebooks   *South Wales*, Reginald Hammond (Ward Lock)
Pembrokeshire, Brian Jones (David and Charles)

Starting point   Llanelli

One of the great pleasures of cycling is the sense of exploration, that little tingle of anticipation that comes with swinging into the saddle and just heading off down the open road. The sensation is always heightened if the tour is to somewhere wild, little-known, or simply off the beaten track. Even in densely populated Britain such places are not hard to find if you study a map and look for the emptier counties.

Pembrokeshire has vanished from most modern maps to be replaced by the newly invented county of Dyfed but, locally at least, Pembrokeshire refuses to die. But then, it's a stubborn sort of place, rugged, wave-beaten, very historic and only half Welsh.

When the Normans came to Wales, in about 1080, they noticed that the south of what became Pembroke was rich and fertile, while the north was rocky and barren, so they simply took over the best places. The Earls of Pembroke were English, and the southern half of the county is noticeably more English than the northern end. North of the 'Landsker' line along the Brandy Brook in St Bride's Bay you are in the Welsh part of Pembroke, with Welsh placenames; even the people speak Welsh. This is a little-known part of Britain and all the better for it. The terrain is rather hilly and the winds seem constant, but there is plenty of accommodation and roads are fairly empty.

This tour begins with a 15-mile ride north from Llanelli on the B4309, a rolling road to Carmarthen. The Romans built their most westerly fort here, Caer Maridunum, and in the eleventh century the Normans came, building a castle which was enlarged and extended by Edward I who walled the town against the incessant raids by the native population. Carmarthen today remains a medieval town, with narrow, winding streets, although only parts of the old walls and a gatehouse now remain.

The route aims to stay as close to the coast as possible, so ride out to the south on the B4312, which runs down the western side of the Tywi estuary to the village of Llanstephan (8 miles). Llanstephan is a surprise in this region of mostly medieval towns, for it is full of elegant Georgian and Victorian houses which line the High Street and lead up to the Square where, inevitably, the church has a Norman tower. The Green, surrounded by colour-washed houses, is overlooked by the ruins of a Norman castle. Then turn west, on a narrow road, across the headland to St Clears (9 miles) on the river Taf. This is, or was, a Norman town with a very fine church, and here you pick up a quiet major road, the A4066, and follow it to Pendine (8 miles) on the coast. The beach at Pendine is a vast expanse of sand, and indeed the whole shoreline of Carmarthen Bay is fringed by fine beaches, perfect for bathing. At Pendine pick up a minor road and follow it around Saundersfoot Bay and into the town of Tenby (12 miles).

Tenby is a Georgian seaside resort with a high, rocky foreshore, which drops down to beaches which are wide and sandy when the tide is out. Part of the town is still walled, and it has the usual ruined castle and an excellent museum. The two 'musts' in Tenby are a visit to the Tudor Merchant's House and a trip out into the bay to visit Caldey Island, which takes about twenty minutes. Caldey has been a religious centre for almost a thousand years and is now owned by a small group of monks, the Cistercians of the Strict Observance or Trappists, who farm and make perfume.

Leave Tenby for the west, again along a minor road, the Ridgeway, with a diversion down to the coast to see the great castle at Manorbier, 6 miles to the west. Built at the end of the thirteenth century, it never saw battle and is in very good state of preservation; it is open to the public daily in summer. Return across the main road and turn west for Lamphey (5 miles) and the town of Pembroke (2 miles).

Pembroke Castle, built in about 1200, is superb. Henry Tudor, later Henry VII, was born in the town in 1457, and Cromwell himself

ABOVE The port of New Quay, Dyfed. BELOW Manorbier Castle, Dyfed.

captured the castle during the Civil War. Pembroke Dock was built at the end of the Napoleonic Wars and remained a naval base for over a century. On the far side of the estuary lies the town of Milford Haven, once, like Pembroke, a lively port, and the great divided estuary which runs inland for many miles, up to Haverfordwest, has always offered safe anchorage for shipping.

Cross the bridge here, and turn west for Milford Haven itself (6 miles) and then out, on minor roads, to the fishing port of Dale (14 miles) on St Ann's Head, with its sailing centre. There are castles on the way and out to sea lies Stack Fort, built to defend the estuary against the French. Mill Bay, close by, is where Henry Tudor landed before marching to defeat Richard III at Bosworth Field in 1485. Out in Broad Sound lies the island of Skokholm, a bird sanctuary, which can be visited in summer.

From Dale ride north to the other, western, arm of this peninsula, jutting out into St Bride's Bay, to Wooltack Point (8 miles) and another bird island, Skomer, before returning, through Marloes (2 miles) on to the B4321 and up to Broad Haven (6 miles). The countryside here is very beautiful, open and spacious, with low hills stretching up behind the long beaches. St Bride's Bay looks due west and the sunsets are often spectacular. This is good walking country and the coastline is followed by the Pembrokeshire Coast Path, one of the longest footpaths in Britain.

The route continues around the great sweep of St Bride's Bay, past Roch Castle and the airfield at Brawdy and down to the smallest city in Britain, St David's (15 miles) on the northern peninsula. All it takes to make a city is a cathedral, and this one is a vast red stone building, tucked out of sight in the deep valley of the river Alun, and best seen from the gatehouse at the 'city' above. St David, the patron saint of Wales, founded a monastery here in the sixth century, but the present cathedral dates from the twelfth century, and contains the saint's shrine and the grave of the chronicler Geraldus Cambrensis. Close by, just across the river, lie the ruins of the huge Archbishop's Palace.

St David's is a romantic place set in a beautiful coastline. One excursion from here is to Ramsey Island, reached after a lively boat ride through the rocks of the Bitches Reef. Another is the walk around Whitesand Bay to St David's Head, before taking the minor roads north and east across country on the B4330 and then out to Strumble Head and the port of Fishguard (25 miles). Another much under-rated town, Fishguard is marred on the surface by the ferry terminal for Ireland. It is, incidentally, the scene of the last invasion of Britain, when a force of 1200 French were defeated here by the local militia during the Napoleonic Wars, and signed a peace treaty in the bar of the Royal Oak. Where better?

From Fishguard the A487 runs north to the next main stop, but avoid it by heading inland on the B4313, then turning north to swing round to Newport (10 miles) by the minor road through Cilgwyn, and so to one of the least-known and most attractive places in Wales. Newport, a coastal village overlooked by a Norman castle, is full of pleasant houses painted pink, blue and green, lining a narrow lane which runs down to the old harbour. It is a restful place, and if you have ridden this far against the westerly winds you will find it a good place to take a day off. From here the B4582 runs up to Cardigan (16 miles) on the river Teifi. It was once a port, but the river has silted up, and not much remains of the castle, or of St Dogmael's Abbey, which lies a mile west of the town and dates from 1115.

From Cardigan take the B4548 up to Gwbert (2 miles), and then wander north, always on that minor road that runs between the coastline and the main A487, through Aberporth, Llangranog and up to New Quay (18 miles), popular in summer and therefore crowded, but beautiful at any time, a small place with a fine unspoiled collection of Georgian and Victorian houses overlooking the minute harbour. The climate seems mild even for this sunny coast, and palm trees flourish. The road rises and falls, wandering into many attractive hamlets, and side roads lead from these places west to the sea.

The temptation now is to carry on along the coast, dropping in on more of these delightful villages. But to complete your tour of Pembrokeshire you must turn south now and head inland to look at the interior of the county, which is very different from the coast.

Take the B4342 from New Quay to Ystrad Aeron, then the A482 and B4337 to Cribyn (12 miles). Cross over two main roads and, still following the B4337, begin a hard ride south, over a hilly route marked only by lone houses or scattered hamlets all the way to Llandeilo (17 miles). Then, still on minor roads, the B4300 and the B4310, head south-west to Port Antwn (14 miles), to the point on the B4309 passed at the start of this tour, and so at last back to Llanelli (10 miles).

This is a splendid one-week tour for a fit cycle tourist. However those who decide to linger on the way and take two weeks for this journey will not regret their decision.

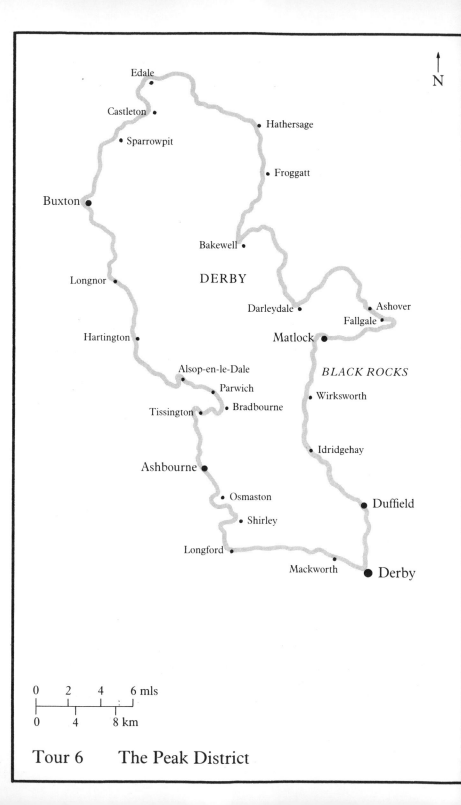

N

Edale

Castleton

Sparrowpit

Hathersage

Froggatt

Buxton

Bakewell

DERBY

Longnor

Darleydale

Ashover

Fallgale

Hartington

Matlock

BLACK ROCKS

Alsop-en-le-Dale

Parwich

Wirksworth

Tissington

Bradbourne

Idridgehay

Ashbourne

Osmaston

Duffield

Shirley

Longford

Mackworth

Derby

0	2	4	6 mls
0	4	8 km	

Tour 6   The Peak District

TOUR 6

The Peak District

I would love you all the day,
Every night would kiss and play,
If with me you'd fondly stray,
Over the hills and far away.
JOHN GAY, *The Beggar's Opera*

Distance 158 miles
Time One week
County Derbyshire
Maps GT Series No.4 (Midlands)
National Series No.24 (Derby and Nottingham), No.29 (The Peak and South Yorkshire)
Guidebooks *The Peak District Companion*, Rex Bellamy (David and Charles)
Visitor's Guide to the Peak District, Lindsey Porter (Moorland Publishing)
The Yorkshire Dales and The Peak District, W.A. Poacher (Constable)
Starting point Derby

The Peak District is one of my favourite places. It's an enclosed up-and-down sort of country, hard to know but easy to like. The terrain is hilly, the roads narrow and winding, running across stone-walled fields down into narrow valleys, with steep, sharp rock faces jutting up here and there. The villages are small and solid and the towns busy, while the hills rear up everywhere.

It is the perfect place for a cycle tour, for it is well supplied with camp sites, youth hostels, small hotels, bed and breakfasts and holiday lets. Apart from the scenery, the great attraction of the Peak District is the people. They may not be the easiest people in the world, but they are friendly. The Peak District is a rugged place which breeds tough, self-reliant people, and they know what they have here – a rare little region of great beauty, one well worth getting to know.

Because of the hills one low gear of 30 ins or less would be useful, and as the weather can be chilly in spring and autumn, it is advisable to take windproofs and some warm clothing. In summer the narrow roads can get very crowded, so, if possible, tour here in the late spring or early autumn.

The Peak District is very compact, plentifully seamed with small, tempting minor roads, so that any tour becomes more a matter of drifting from point to point than sticking rigidly to a fixed itinerary. This tour is simply the route followed on my travels; it took me to most of the main sights of the region and left me wanting to return. There are plenty more places to visit if you wish to stay longer.

Derby is an industrial town, much rebuilt in recent years. It has a fine range of outdoor shops which cycle campers will enjoy visiting, but it is probably best to leave the town as quickly as possible and ride north-west up the A52 towards Ashbourne (15 miles), turning left at Mackworth and taking very minor roads into the Peak, and right after Longford to Rodsley and the village of Shirley. Shirley is a good introduction to the Peak villages, a very neat place with a huge yew tree in the graveyard of St Michael's church. It is quite easy to get lost in the maze of lanes around here, but if you go south-west you will pick up the lane leading north to Osmaston and so down the hill into the little town of Ashbourne. This is the gateway to the Peak, a market town with a cobbled market square and St Oswald's church, the 'Cathedral of the Peak', which was much admired by the nineteenth-century novelist George Eliot.

Ride north of here and pick up the Tissington Trail, a footpath and cycleway which follows the old railway line and is therefore gently graded, or pick up the minor road that drops down to the Manifold valley, up to Astonfield – and that's the snag with the Peak, there is such a choice of route. Tissington (3 miles) is a picture-book village and a centre for the curious custom of well dressing, when the local wells are decorated with beautiful designs made from flower petals, a custom said to date back to the Black Death in 1349. The Tissington well dressing ceremony takes place on Ascension Day, when five local wells, Yewtree, Hall Well, Hands Well, Coffin Well and Town Well, are framed with flowers pressed into clay to make biblical scenes.

The Tissington Trail runs through here from Ashbourne to Buxton and offers some splendid views of the countryside along the way. Heading east from Tissington, cross the ford and turn up the B5056 for Bradbourne (3 miles), which has an eighth-century Saxon cross in the churchyard of All Saints. Bradbourne is a quiet, rather lonely village, and from here there is a pleasant ride up to the heights at Minninglow Hill near Ballidon (2 miles), before returning to Bradbourne and taking another minor road to Parwich and Alsop-en-le-Dale (3 miles). Parwich is set in the green Peak hills, and Alsop dates back to Norman times. Just south of Alsop, on the A515, a small road runs down to Alstonfield and north into the village of Hartington (6 miles).

Here you will find a good hotel, the Charles Cotton, which recalls the famous fisherman who took Izaak Walton fishing in the Dove Valley nearby. There is also a youth hostel and a dairy which produces excellent Stilton cheese. The youth hostel at Hartington Hall sheltered Bonnie Prince Charlie in 1745, and the church of St Giles is well worth a visit. Hartington is a good centre for riding or walking down to the Dove Valley, arguably the most attractive valley in the Peak. Before leaving Hartington, which would make a good night stop and a base for a day's ride around, visit Arbor Low, a stone circle near the A515, and take a walk down into Dovedale.

The Dove tinkles over the stones in the valley to the right as you ride up to Longnor (4 miles) on the B5053, on to the A515 for a brief time, and then into the spa town of Buxton (5 miles). It is a very old town, but many of the present elegant buildings owe their existence to the fifth Duke of Devonshire, who built the baths and the assembly rooms in the eighteenth and early nineteenth centuries. Although the baths are now closed, the town still gets plenty of visitors.

Heading north, ride the A6 for 5 miles, leave Chapel-en-le-Frith to the west, and then ride on to the B6061 to the windy heights of Mam Tor (4 miles), crowned by an Iron Age fort. A popular spot for hang gliding, it gives superb views over the Edale Valley, the Pennines ahead, and Castleton far below. Castleton lies in the limestone White Peak area and is noted as a caving centre. There are many caverns in the hills, and four of them can be visited.

From Castleton take the minor road to the north along the river Noe and through the Vale of Edale, at the start of the Pennine Way (2 miles). Continue east back to the A625 and ride round to Hathersage (7 miles), set in the gritstone country, with Millstone Edge to the south and Stonage Edge to the north. There is a very long grave in the churchyard at Hathersage which is said to be that of Robin Hood's

OVERLEAF Near Mam Tor, Derbyshire.

comrade, Little John. The vicarage was featured by Charlotte Brontë in *Jane Eyre*; certainly there are memorials to the Eyre family in the church at Hathersage, which looks very brooding when the evening draws shadows down the valley.

From Hathersage take the B6001 to Froggatt (3 miles). Then pick up the A623 for 2 miles, turning south on the B6012 to the great house of Chatsworth (5 miles), home of the Dukes of Devonshire. Even those who don't much care for great houses will enjoy this one. The gardens were created by Joseph Paxton (1803–65), who spent most of his life at Chatsworth and designed, among other pleasures, the gravity-fed Emperor Fountain. The greenhouses here pre-date Paxton's Crystal Palace, erected for the 1851 Exhibition. He also laid out the nearby village of Edensor where he lies buried, no doubt worn out by his many endeavours. Chatsworth, the Palace of the Peak, was built originally for the formidable Bess of Hardwick, who lived here from 1549. On her death the house went to her second son, William, the first Duke of Devonshire. Very little is left of Bess's creation, for the house was rebuilt in the early eighteenth century and the park landscaped by Capability Brown.

Now ride on to Bakewell (3 miles), famous for tarts and Jane Austen, who lived here while writing *Pride and Prejudice*. Though attractive, it need not detain you long, unlike Ashford-in-the-Water, a perfect gem 2 miles to the west. The water is the river Wye, and the stone bridge across it is notable for including a sheep dip.

Five miles to the north of Bakewell lies the plague village of Eyam. It's a remote place, and when the Great Plague arrived here in 1665, the villagers elected to stay and die rather than flee and risk spreading the infection throughout the county. It is estimated that some 250 of the 350 villagers died. Their graves are dotted all over the village, but don't let that depress you. It's a cheerful spot today and the well dressing here, on the last Saturday in August, is said to be the best in Derbyshire.

The A6 gives a swift ride south to Darleydale (3 miles), where the B5057 turns left for a little diversion across the Amber, towards the Red Lion Inn, then a sharp turn and down to Ashover (7 miles), centre of an unspoilt valley, with a fine pub, the Crispin. Cut across by Fallgate to the B6014 and turn west for Matlock and Matlock Bath (6 miles), another spa, in the deep valley of the river Derwent.

Matlock, Derbyshire.

From here take to the A6 briefly to the crossroads at Black Rocks, and then cross over on to the B5036 to Wirksworth (4 miles), a centre for the Derbyshire lead mining industry, then on for 3 miles to another little-known village, Idridgehay, on the southern edge of the Peak. There is a good pub here, the Black Swan, and plenty of good architecture, but the chief attraction, for me at least, is the village setting amid green hills and golden meadows. From here it is possible to avoid the heavy traffic and remain on the B5023 all the way south to the outskirts of Derby at Duffield (6 miles), and the end of this journey.

This is a fairly short tour which could be accomplished in a long weekend if you were pushed for time. Personally I would take longer if possible, in order to visit Chatsworth and Eyam, walk along the Dove, or just sit on hilltops and enjoy the views.

Peveril Castle, near Castleton, Derbyshire.

TOUR 7

The Yorkshire Moors and Dales

Yorkshire was not English – or else all England, as the Yorkshiremen might choose to express it.
HENRY ADAMS, *The Education of Henry Adams*

Distance   297 miles

Time   One week

County   North Yorkshire

Maps   GT No.6 (North England)
National Series No.32 (West Yorkshire), No.33 (York and Humberside), No.35 (Darlington and North Yorkshire), No.36 (Teesside and Yorkshire Moors)

Guidebooks   *A Visitor's Guide to the Yorkshire Dales*, Brian Spencer (Moorland Publishing)
Portrait of Yorkshire, H. J. Scott (Hale)
The Yorkshire Dales, Peter Gunn (Century)

Starting point   York

Any book of cycle tours in Britain has to include a trip to Yorkshire, but there is such a large number of places to visit in the county that it is hard to choose. Yorkshire folk are never reluctant to sing the praises of their home and the stranger will not be there long before realizing that there is a lot to sing about. Yorkshire, and I refer here to the large ancient county divided into Ridings rather than the present partition into North, South and West Yorkshire, Cleveland and Humberside, is a big place and it takes time to see even a part of it.

Presenting a tour that displays the diversity and charm of Yorkshire is no easy task. The tour I have described here is not the one I originally planned, and leaves out many diversions which travellers with more time might like to add to their journey.

In the end, I have opted for a route in what is now North Yorkshire, which takes in the North York Moors, visits the coastline between Scarborough and Whitby, then makes a great sweep across the Dales, and so returns to historic York, visiting many other places on the way.

The terrain is varied, and fairly up and down across the moors and

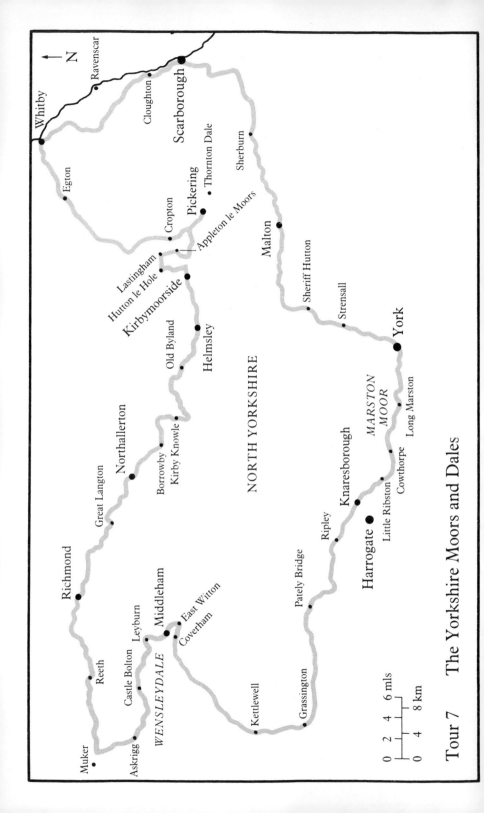

Tour 7 The Yorkshire Moors and Dales

dales, although with a little judicious planning it is possible to follow the rivers and reduce the climbing. I also recall rather a lot of days battling into a headwind, but neither weather nor terrain present any real obstacle. There is plenty of accommodation, although if you are going in the summer months it is wise to book ahead.

York is a splendid city, so allow a day to see it before you set out. The old streets are narrow, crowded, and often cobbled, so leave your bike somewhere safe and explore it on foot, being sure to see the Minster, the marvellous Railway Museum and the newly excavated Jorvik Viking City, and wander around such places as the Shambles, Stonegate and the strangely named Whip-ma-Whop-ma Gate, where thieves were flogged in the Middle Ages.

Leave on the A64, turning north a short distance from the city centre on to a minor road that leads north into open country and to Huntington, Strensall and Sheriff Hutton (10 miles), heading for the great attraction in North Yorkshire, the splendid country house called Castle Howard (7 miles). It was built by Vanbrugh and work started in 1700, though Vanbrugh had died before it was completed in 1737. The castle is an artistic treasure house and the gardens and lake are magnificent.

Five miles to the west lies Malton, a very attractive market town, from which it is a full day's run east along the A64 to Scarborough (25 miles). This road can be busy but the land is fairly flat, and follows the Derwent for much of the way. A popular seaside resort, Scarborough lies in a splendid setting with a great Norman castle on the clifftop, a picturesque harbour still full of trawlers, and several fine churches, including the medieval St Mary's where Anne Brontë is buried.

Leave Scarborough for a tour north on the Yorkshire coastline, first on the A165 and A171 , turning right at Cloughton for Ravenscar, set on high cliffs with great views across the North Sea, then back again on to the A171 to Robin Hood's Bay and into the fishing port of Whitby (25 miles) on the river Esk. An abbey stood here, of which the ruins remain, and Captain Cook sailed in a Whitby ship, the *Endeavour*, on his first voyage round the world.

Heading west, follow the A171 for 3 miles, then turn off on a minor road to the south for Egton, and a long, hard, windy ride across the moor, past Egton Pike at 1071 ft and then into Rosedale by the river Seven. Follow the road down through Cropton and into Pickering (29 miles), a market town for the North York Moors, and at the southern end of the North Yorkshire Moors Railway, a private steam line which runs for 18 miles up to Grossmont in Eskdale, a very enjoyable excursion with superb views.

Thornton Dale, 2 miles east of Pickering, is an attractive village with Georgian houses and a fine line of seventeenth-century alms-houses set on the slopes above Thornton beck, but the cyclist's route, the A170, lies to the west, past the Cropton turn, then right up to Appleton le Moor, Lastingham and Hutton le Hole, both worth this diversion off the A170. In Lastingham's High Street is a well, recalling the fact that a Celt, St Cedd, founded an abbey here in 654. There is also a good pub, the Blacksmith's Arms, and a very fine church, St Mary's.

Hutton le Hole is bigger, and the classic village of the North York Moors. Mentioned in Domesday Book, it was a home for persecuted Quakers in the seventeenth century, but above all, as so often here on the moors, it's the look of the place and its setting that provides the attraction. Small bridges cross the beck, and bright green hills soar up on either side. From here, narrow lanes lead off the moor to the village of Kirbymoorside (11 miles) on the A170. Then go west to Helmsley (6 miles), once the home of Charles I's great favourite, the Duke of Buckingham, who lived in Helmsley Castle; most of the castle is now in ruins as, alas, is nearby Rievaulx Abbey, in the woods of Ryedale. Rievaulx was a Cistercian foundation, and had over six hundred monks in its heyday before it was dissolved by Henry VIII.

From Rievaulx minor roads and lanes run west, threading their way through a wonderful landscape dotted with farms and hamlets. It is easy to get lost, but my route is through Old Byland, Kirby Knowle and Borrowby up to Northallerton (25 miles), a surprisingly large, and busy town after the peace of the open moors. Leave quickly.

The B6271 turns off the A167 in the northern outskirts of Northallerton and takes you to Great Langton, a lovely ride across the A1 and into the historic town of Richmond (18 miles), gateway to the Dales and one of the finest towns in Yorkshire. A great castle overlooks the town, which has a vast market place fed by narrow cobbled alleys known as wynds. There is an interesting museum devoted to the local regiment, the Green Howards, a theatre and fine walks along the river Swale, well worth an extended stop.

OPPOSITE ABOVE The port of Whitby.

BELOW A view of the Yorkshire Dales.

Leave by the minor road which runs north of the Swale, west to the village of Marske (5 miles), and on to Reeth (4 miles) and Grinton, at the point where Swaledale meets the northern valley of Arkengarthdale. Follow Swaledale down to Muker (8 miles), before turning south over the moor and into the southern valley, Wensleydale, at Askrigg (5 miles). Here turn east, still on the minor road, for Castle Bolton (7 miles). Turn off south on the way here to Aysgarth, for a view of the spectacular falls at Aysgarth Force (1 mile). The carriage museum here was once a mill which wove the red cloth for the shirts of the nineteenth-century Italian revolutionaries, led by Garibaldi.

Castle Bolton lies above Wensleydale. It is a steep ride up to the village where the only street leads up to the castle, built by Richard Scrope in the fourteenth century and later a prison for Mary, Queen of Scots. The main hall of the castle is now a restaurant.

From here the route runs east towards Wensley and Leyburn (5 miles), where you should take the A6108 south to Middleham (2 miles), a centre for racehorse stables – if you get up early you can see long lines of horses being ridden out for exercise. The village, which contains plenty to see, is crowned by Middleham Castle, which belonged to Warwick the Kingmaker and then to Richard III. Ride south for 4 miles to the romantic ruins of Jervaulx Abbey, the place where Cistercian monks created Wensleydale cheese.

I prefer to avoid main roads, so I suggest you cut west at East Witton, on the way back, for Coverham (3 miles). Turn south there on a long ride across the open moors to Kettlewell (15 miles), a wild little place, and the high spot on the moor; Great Whernside, just to the east, stands at 2310 ft. This is climbing country and full of attractive crags. From this high point the road falls to Grassington (6 miles) and turns east on the B6265 to Pateley Bridge (12 miles), then on the B6165 to Ripley (8 miles), a curious place to find in Yorkshire. It was rebuilt in 1827 by a local eccentric, to resemble a village in Alsace in eastern France. The church is much older and still bears the bullet marks where Royalist prisoners were shot after the Battle of Marston Moor in 1644. To the south lies Harrogate (3 miles), a famous centre for cyclists, and a spa and conference town. My preferred route skirts Harrogate and takes the B6165 into Knaresborough (4 miles), then out on the B6164 and, after 4 miles, left on a minor road to Long Marston (9 miles), with the battlefield of Marston Moor on the left. From Long Marston the B1224 leads east, back again after 7 miles into the city of York.

TOUR 8

A Tour of East Anglia

A large country it is, and full of havens.
WILLIAM CAMDEN, *Britain*

Distance   348 miles

Time   Two weeks

Counties   Cambridgeshire, Norfolk, Suffolk, Essex

Maps   GT No.5 (East Anglia)
National Series No.26 (Norfolk), No.21 (Suffolk), No.16 (Essex)

Guidebooks   *Companion Guide to East Anglia*, John Seymour (Collins)
Visitor's Guide to East Anglia, Clive Tully (Moorland Publishing)
East Anglian Journey, Michael Watkins (East Anglian Magazine)

Starting point   Cambridge

East Anglia has always been a popular area for cycle touring, probably because it is reputed to be flat: 'Very flat, Norfolk', as the saying goes. In fact while Cambridgeshire is certainly flat, Norfolk and Suffolk have their fair share of hills, although in general the terrain is fairly gentle and good daily mileages quite possible. There is no lack of good accommodation, although it pays to book at weekends or in holiday periods.

The winds blow in across the North Sea, so this tour runs north and south, in the hope that the wind will not always be head-on and make the pedalling hard work. This tour begins in the university town of Cambridge.

Cambridge is easily reached by train and no great distance from London by road if you want to cycle up to the start of the tour. The city itself offers much to see and do, so allow a day at least here. Take a trip along the river Cam to see the Backs, and ride out for tea at Grantchester, made famous by Rupert Brooke, or north to the

Tour 8   A Tour of East Anglia

cathedral city of Ely, 16 miles away in the Fens, a pleasant trip for the afternoon and early evening.

On the next day start by leaving on the A1303, turning north-east on the B1102 for Burwell and Mildenhall (22 miles), before taking the B1112 for Lakenheath and Methwold (14 miles), skirting the Fens. To the north-east is Swaffham, which stands on one of the few hills hereabouts and has two fine churches, twelfth-century St Mary's and thirteenth-century St Cyriac's. Turn left at Wrenton to avoid the A134, and the first major stop is the attractive little town of Downham Market (8 miles), a centre for local farmers and a link between the Fen country and Norfolk.

Follow the A10 to Wimbotsham (1 mile), then take the minor road to the west which runs up through Watlington and a number of quiet villages to the town of King's Lynn (16 miles) on the river Ouse. Lynn, as the locals call it, is an old town and was featured in the Domesday Book; it is worth an overnight stop. King John gave the town its charter before he lost the Crown Jewels crossing the Wash, but it was Henry VIII who gave it the 'royal' prefix. The glory of Lynn is its architecture: there are fine buildings everywhere of every period from the fifteenth century to the present, an indication of continuous local prosperity. The medieval guildhall of Lynn is the oldest surviving guildhall in England. On leaving, follow the A1078 for South Wooton, then turn left on a minor road, later the B1439, for Castle Rising (4 miles), once a port and still overlooked by a well-preserved Norman keep. The almshouses, endowed in 1614 by the Howards, support twelve ladies who to this day can be seen going to church wearing red cloaks which display the Howard coat-of-arms.

Follow the B1439 up to the royal estate of Sandringham, and then take the minor road to Docking (10 miles) and up to Burnham Market (6 miles), on the north Norfolk coast. Close by lies the small village of Burnham Thorpe, the birthplace of the victor of Trafalgar, Horatio, Viscount Nelson, who was born in the vicarage. The church, and Nelson Hall, contain relics of Nelson, and the church lectern is made of wood from his flagship, HMS *Victory*.

Passing through Burnham Thorpe and turning inland, the route leads down to the shrine of Our Lady of Walsingham (9 miles), which has attracted pilgrims since 1061. The medieval church was destroyed by Henry VIII, but a replica was built in the 1930s, and the pilgrims returned, attracted by the relics, including two pieces of the True Cross.

The Backs, Cambridge.

Heading back to the coast, a small road becomes the B1388 and leads through Langham to Blakeney and Cley (12 miles). The church at Blakeney has a tower 100 ft high, a local landmark for sailors when Blakeney was a port. The quay still looks out to sea across the marshes. Five miles away lies Cley-next-the-Sea, now actually a mile inland. Cley has a windmill, many old brick and flint buildings, a steep shingle beach and a bird sanctuary. The fine memorial brasses of the merchants in St Mary's church indicate the former prosperity of this little coastal port. Before leaving this part of Norfolk you can ride 2 miles west to the village of Stiffkey, made famous in the 1920s by its unfortunate vicar, who managed to get first unfrocked and then eaten by a lion.

To the east lie Sheringham and then Cromer (11 miles), a great place for seafood and a popular seaside resort. From here take the B1436 inland, branching off through Thurgarton and Blickling for the fine city of Norwich (28 miles). Blickling Manor once belonged to the Saxon King Harold and later to Sir John Falstaff. The present Jacobean house in red brick was built about 1616. From here, pick up the B1149 for Norwich, which is well worth an extended stop. There is a fine cathedral begun in 1096 and frequently embellished, a castle dating from the mid twelfth century and many old buildings. Norwich claims to have a pub for every other day of the year and a church for every Sunday, but it is also the gateway to the Broads, that vast region of fen and waterway that lies between it and Great Yarmouth to the east. Wroxham, 6 miles north-east, is a great boating centre.

Enjoy a full day and an overnight stop in Norwich, then take the A146 south, turning right after a mile on to the B1332 and south for 15 miles to Bungay on the Suffolk border, then the A1116 for Beccles (6 miles), from where the quiet B1127 leads south to the coast at Southwold (14 miles), a lovely village with a marvellous church dedicated to St Edmund, built about 1430. It contains a wooden effigy called Southwold Jack, who begins each service by striking a bell with his sword.

From Southwold take the B1387 and the 1125 to Westleton (8 miles), then the B1122 to Aldeburgh (11 miles), and the Maltings at Snape, home of the music festival, before turning north for Sax-mundham (8 miles) and Framlingham (7 miles). Framlingham is one of those underrated places with a lot to see, including a great castle dating from just after the Norman Conquest, which was for centuries the home of the Bigods, the first Earls of Norfolk. The church of St Michael, beside the castle, commemorates the Howards, the later Dukes of Norfolk, with some fine carvings.

Turn south for Wickham Market (6 miles) and then continue east, on the B1078 and A1141, through Needham Market for Lavenham (27 miles). Lavenham was a centre for the East Anglian wool trade, which rivalled that of the Cotswolds, and the fine church here dates from that plentiful period in the fifteenth century. Much photographed and used in the making of historical television programmes, Lavenham's half-timbered high street is a picturesque prelude to the charms of the Constable country, now only a short distance away.

Long Melford, a few miles to the west, has an exceptionally long and well-preserved main street with many fine eighteenth-century town houses alongside much older timber-framed cottages. In this area many surprisingly large flint churches will be seen, a legacy from the prosperous days of the wool trade, and Melford Church, light and airy, is thought to be one of the best examples. Across the green is Melford Hall, an impressive red-brick Elizabethan house with an interior that was almost totally remodelled in Regency times. Five miles further to the west, via Cavendish on the A1092, is the small town of Clare, famous for its old plastered houses embellished with the local form of freehand moulding known as pargetting, as well as a ruined castle and priory.

From Clare meander south-east on narrow lanes through the villages known as the Belchamps to Sudbury (10 miles), a busy market town and home of the artist Thomas Gainsborough, whose modest house is now a museum. Take the A134 and B1068 south-east again to Stoke by Nayland, a large, peaceful village graced with another huge wool church, then Thorington Street and Higham. This corner of Suffolk is particularly unspoilt, and forays in a northerly direction between Stoke and Thorington Street are rewarding if surprisingly hilly.

Cross the A12, following signs for East Bergholt, where John Constable was born, in the Stour valley. The bells for East Bergholt church are not in the belfry, but in an unusual bellhouse in the churchyard. Take the narrow lane down to Flatford Mill and Willy Lott's Cottage, made famous by Constable's paintings, and a very crowded spot in summer. For the last leg of the tour, go east to the A137 and after Lawford take a detour round the pretty village of Dedham before riding down the B1029 and A137 to the old Roman town of Colchester.

The river Ouse at Ely.

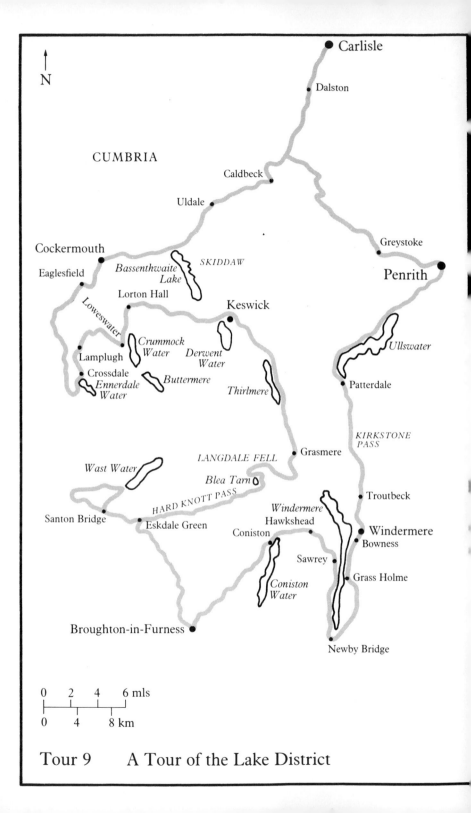

Tour 9   A Tour of the Lake District

TOUR 9

A Tour of the Lake District

I do not know any tract of country in which, in so narrow a compass, may be found an equal variety in the influence of light and shadow upon the sublime and beautiful features of the landscape.
WILLIAM WORDSWORTH

Distance   226 miles

Time   One week

County   Cumbria

Maps   GT No.6 (North England)
National Series No.38 (Carlisle and Solway), No.34 (Lake District)

Guidebooks   *Portrait of the Lakes*, Norman Nicolson (Hale)
A Visitor's Guide to the Lake District, Brian Spencer (Moorland Publishing)
Portrait of Cumbria, J. D. Marshall (Hale)
Cycling in the Lake District, R. D. Harris (Moorland Publishing)

Starting point   Carlisle

The Lake District is rightly famous as one of the most beautiful parts of Britain. Even the region's more recent role as a popular tourist centre has been unable to spoil the attractions and natural splendour created by this combination of lakes and mountains. Many people wax lyrical about the Lakes, and, return there as often as you will, the first impression on every visit is always breathtaking.

This tour circles south and west across the Lake District, visiting all the main lakes and many of the minor ones, circling the highest fells and using minor roads whenever possible. In summer and other peak holiday periods, the roads through the Lake District can be crowded, but the views are so marvellous that motorists don't drive fast, so even the main roads are never dangerous. Accommodation of all kinds, from luxury hotel to campsite, is plentiful, although in high season it would certainly pay to book ahead.

The Lake District has always been popular with walkers and

climbers, and you would be well advised to leave your bike for at least a day and walk to the crest of one of the fells, taking all due care and keeping an eye on the weather. The fact has to be faced that in the Lakes it rains, sometimes for days on end, so good waterproofs are advisable.

The area could just as well be called the Fell District, for the hills are beautiful and the roads frequently steep. The Hard Knott, Wrynose and Kirkstone passes may call for walking. At least one low gear of 30 ins or less will be very useful, certainly to cycle campers, but the climbs are rewarded by fine views at the top and long glides to the lakes below.

Carlisle is an ancient fortress town which has been a battleground for centuries, from the days of the Romans to Bonnie Prince Charlie in 1745. The castle is worth a visit; among the many people detained within its walls was Mary, Queen of Scots, and the Jacobite prisoners captured in the '45 Rebellion. Today it contains the museum of the Border Regiment. The cathedral was well restored in the nineteenth century.

Leave Carlisle by the B5299 for Dalston (4 miles), and follow this road until the turning for Caldbeck (8 miles), an attractive village with buildings of grey-green stone, where the churchyard contains the grave of the famous huntsman John Peel, who died in 1854 after falling from his horse. Peel apart, Caldbeck is the perfect place to start a tour of the Lake District, offering fine views to the south.

Leave Caldbeck by the road that leads past Parkend and continue to Uldale (6 miles), then on a rising road to Bassenthwaite and Skiddaw, rising 3053 ft to the south, a fine sight on a clear, cold afternoon. There is a big lake below Bassenthwaite, but continue to Cockermouth (6 miles), where Wordsworth was born in 1770, turning south on minor roads through Eaglesfield to Ennerdale Water and the Anglers Inn (15 miles). Ennerdale is one of the smaller lakes, less frequently visited than the more popular ones to the east, but beautiful for all that and crowned at the south end by the bulk of Ennerdale Fell.

Turn north again here, through Lamplugh, to join the Mockerkin to Loweswater road, on Crummock Water (12 miles). Four miles

OPPOSITE Honister Pass in the Lake District.

OVERLEAF Ullswater.

south, on the eastern edge of the lake, lies Buttermere village, but you should turn north on the B5289 for Lorton Hall, then east to Keswick at the head of Derwentwater (8 miles). If you stay in Keswick you might try the circular tour round Derwentwater and Buttermere on the B5289. Keswick is a popular tourist town, usually crowded, so after looking at the lake take the A591 and ride south down Thirlmere with Helvellyn (3118 ft) rising to the left, all the way to Wordsworth's cottage at Grasmere (16 miles).

Dove Cottage at Grasmere, where Wordsworth and his sister lived for nine years, can be visited on most days in summer. The exhibits include his manuscripts, photographs and portraits, as well as his straw hat and walking boots – Wordsworth and his friend, the poet Coleridge, were famous walkers and thought nothing of walking 20 miles to post a letter.

West of Grasmere lies some famous walking and climbing country. To see it ride south and then east on a minor road that leads up Langdale Fell, the B5343, to the Dungeon Ghyll Hotel at the foot of Langdale Pikes, and then down, past Blea Tarn, back to the road junction just north of the A593 (10 miles). This marks the start of a great ride, perhaps the most exciting section of this tour, across two famous high passes to Wastwater.

From the road junction, at around 600 ft, the road west climbs through empty country to the Wrynose Pass (1281 ft), and then over the Hard Knott Pass. If you have to walk, don't worry, for these are very steep climbs. Then keep on, south of Eskdale Fell, picking up the course of the river Esk, crossing it at Eskdale Green, and so past Santon Bridge to beautiful Wast Water. The total distance is over 20 miles and, with the views and the odd pub, plus the steep climbs to contend with, this is a section to linger over and enjoy. There is a youth hostel by Wast Water, and several bed and breakfast places.

Return to Eskdale Green and take the minor road south, past Devoke Water to Ulpha and Broughton-in-Furness (15 miles), where you should take the A593 north to Coniston (9 miles). Coniston Water is one of the famous lakes, once much used for water-speed record attempts. A little south of Coniston itself, at Brantwood on the eastern lakeside, is the house once owned by John Ruskin, where, even if the house is closed, the gardens are beautiful. If you feel like a day off have it here, for the scenery is wonderful. From Coniston the B5285 leads over the fell, past Hawkshead, to the next lake to the east, Windermere (9 miles), arriving in the centre of the lake at Sawrey. To the north, out in the lake, lies Belle Isle. The circular house on the island was built in about 1774 by a Mr English who, according to Wordsworth, was the first outsider to settle in the Lake District because of the scenery, a reminder that loving natural beauty for itself is a fairly new idea. Sawrey itself consists of two tiny hamlets, Far Sawrey and Near Sawrey. The latter was the home of Beatrix Potter, who bought Hilltop Farm with the royalties from *Peter Rabbit*.

Turn south here, to start a circuit of the lake, down to Finsthwaite and Newby Bridge (6 miles). Finsthwaite is one of the smallest villages in the Lake District, a beautiful place with a very fine church, surrounded by woods and deep meadows. From Newby Bridge ride round the bottom of the lake and take the minor road to the ruins of Cartmel Priory (5 miles), built in about 1188 by monks of the Augustinian Order. Then descend to the lakeside at Grass Holme and turn north again for Bowness (7 miles).

Bowness-on-Windermere and Windermere itself are quite large places, at least for Lakeland, which is mostly a place of small villages. From here you can take boat trips on the lake, to Ambleside in the north or south to Belle Isle. Since a lake trip is all part of a holiday hereabouts, why not do so before taking the A592 for the pretty village of Troutbeck (3 miles), which has a church with glass by Burne-Jones. From here the road climbs steeply to the top of the Kirkstone Pass (1476 ft), 4 miles to the north, where the Traveller's Rest is said to be the highest inn in the Lake District. From here there is a long descent through Patterdale to the next lake, Ullswater, and down to Penrith, a beautiful run. The total distance from Windermere to Penrith is about 30 miles, so with the various distractions this would make a good full day's run.

Penrith is a busy town on both the A6 and M6, so leave quickly, taking the B5288 for Greystoke (5 miles), which is overlooked by the impressive walls of a medieval castle. Greystoke has a thirteenth-century church, St Andrew's, a fine pub, the Boot and Shoe, and some attractive seventeenth-century cottages. From here the road goes north-west, rising and falling, back to north of Caldbeck (12 miles), to complete this circular tour of the Lake District at the junction with the B5299.

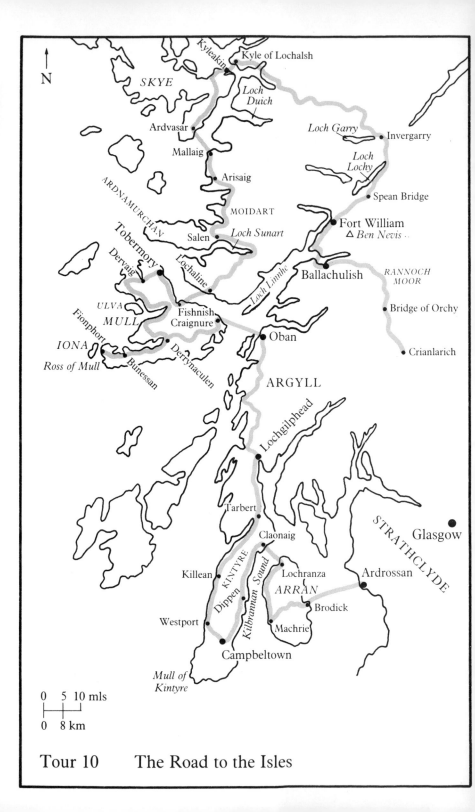

Tour 10   The Road to the Isles

TOUR 10

The Road to the Isles

I had desired to visit the Hebrides, or Western Isles of Scotland, so long, that I scarcely remember how the wish was excited.
SAMUEL JOHNSON, *Journey to the Western Isles of Scotland*

Distance 468 miles

Time Three weeks

Regions Strathclyde, Grampian, Highland

Maps GT No.7 (South West Scotland), No.9 (North West Scotland), No.10 (North East Scotland)
National Series No.44 (Glasgow and the Clyde), No.43 (Islay and Kintyre), No.47 (Oban and Mull), No.50 (Arisaig and Lochaber), No.54 (Skye and Torridon)

Guidebooks *Companion Guide to the West Highlands of Scotland*, W. H. Murray (Collins)
The Highlands and Islands, Francis Thompson (Hale)
Saddle Tramp in the Highlands, Robert Orrell (Hale)
A Journey to the Western Isles, Samuel Johnson (Macdonald)

Starting point Ardrossan

This tour to and through the Western Highlands and Islands of Scotland has to be one of the finest cycle rides in the world, and the bike is, in every sense, the perfect vehicle for this perfect journey. The distances are too long to cover comfortably on foot and a car can be a liability on the narrow Highland roads. Although I recommend three full weeks for this trip to see all the sights, it would be possible to do it in two weeks by riding hard or cutting the tour short after Skye and returning to Glasgow from Mallaig on the West Highland railway line, which crosses some of the most wonderful wild country in Britain.

Various sea crossings will have to be made on the ferries of the Caledonian Macbrayne line, known everywhere in the Highlands as Cal-Mac. If you want to shorten the journey, or gain a little ground by hopping on a local train or finding another ferry crossing, you will miss very little. Remember to keep an eye on the weather, which can be very variable, and check the ferry sailing times carefully at railway stations or tourist offices, for they vary in frequency according to the time of year. The terrain here can be steep, the winds strong, and the roads often rather rough, so plan shorter than normal stages, and accept that there will be days when the weather makes cycling less than enjoyable. Good seasons for this tour are late spring and early summer, and autumn, when the heather is in bloom on the hills.

This is a marvellous tour, but even though it takes in so much, just as much has had to be left out. I have yet to see Castle Stalker or Inveraray, or ride down the Great Glen to Inverness and Culloden, though that is always possible on another occasion. The weather can be difficult, and Rannoch Moor at 1500 ft can be a bleak and dangerous spot, even for cyclists, until well into the spring, but the problems are really very few. Even in summer the roads are uncrowded, and even in spring or autumn the weather can be warm.

Ardrossan is the mainland ferry port for our first island, Arran, and from the castle above the town, destroyed by Cromwell, there are fine views across the Firth of Clyde to Arran and south to the little rock called Ailsa Craig. The ferry ride from Ardrossan to Brodick on Arran takes just under an hour, but take time ashore to see Brodick Castle, home of the Dukes of Hamilton, which has a marvellous rhododendron garden. For a good glimpse of Arran, mountainous in the north but more open to the south, ride west across the island on the road to Machrie (11 miles), and then north on the A841 for the next ferry port at Lochranza (15 miles), a great day's ride with views across the Sound of Kilbrannan to Kintyre.

The ferry crossing to Claonaig takes thirty minutes. On landing take the B842, south to Dippen (12 miles), with a short diversion to the picturesque port of Carradale, and then to Campbeltown, a good place to stay while touring the southern parts of this island. One road leads out of Campbeltown to the south, into the Mull of Kintyre and Southend (10 miles), which makes a pleasant day's ride before leaving for the north on the A83, for a long stretch along the western coast of Kintyre to Tarbert (38 miles), then on to Lochgilphead (12 miles).

Tarbert, on the shores of Loch Fyne, can tell a curious tale, for in 1098 the Scots King Edgar told the Viking, Magnus Barefoot, that he

OPPOSITE ABOVE The hills of Skye.

BELOW Fort William and Ben Nevis.

could possess any island he could sail around in his longship. Magnus already ruled many of the Western Isles but he also wanted Kintyre, so he sat at the tiller of his ship while his men dragged it across the isthmus here and so claimed the 'island' for himself. Today Tarbert is a pretty port, famous for kippers.

North again from Lochgilphead, stay on the A816 for 2 miles, then go west on the B841, down the side of the Crinan Canal, built in the late eighteenth century to carry ships between Loch Fyne and the Atlantic. Now cycle north for 40 miles, along the coast of Argyll into the town of Oban, a busy port where seals frolic by the fishing boats in the harbour. It is possible to join or leave the tour here, heading to or from Glasgow on the West Highland line which runs from Glasgow into Oban.

From Oban, take the Cal-Mac ferry to the island of Mull, a journey of about an hour, to the port of Craignure. Here you should turn south and see Duart Castle, home of the Chief of the MacLeans. Then ride on across the island, through the Great Glen under Ben More, into the Ross of Mull and the little village of Fionphort (30 miles), for the five-minute ferry ride to the little island of Iona, a splendid place for any traveller to visit.

Cars are not permitted on Iona, and you don't really need a bike, for it is a very small place, so you can leave your cycle at a bed and breakfast at Fionphort. Visit the Abbey of St Columba, and walk across the island to the sand dunes, the *machair*, and the great bay facing the Atlantic, a wild and beautiful spot. Iona has a campsite and two small hotels, and wild camping is permitted, although it is as well to ask permission.

Back again on Mull, ride down the Ross for 12 miles, then turn north for a long and marvellous ride on the B8035 and B8073 to Tobermory (34 miles). This western road, which runs past Ulva's Island and Calgary Bay, is a spectacular and unforgettable route. I rode it in January, on a very warm day, without passing another cyclist or even a car until I ran down the hill to Tobermory.

This fine little port, with a whisky distillary, plenty of accommodation, and somewhere in the bay the wreck of a Spanish galleon, is a good place to stop after a hard day's ride. To leave Mull, ride south from Tobermory down the road to Fishnish (10 miles), and take the short ferry trip across the Sound of Mull to Lochaline, in Morvern.

Once ashore, head north on the A884, a steep ride up Glen Geal, to Glen Tarbert (12 miles), turning west down the northern edge of Loch

126

Sunart to Salen (11 miles). This is a wild area, very typical of the Highlands, with the Ardnamurchan peninsula running out to the west and the heather-clad hills of Moidart straddling the road to the north, the A861, which leads around the coast to Arisaig and Mallaig (37 miles), where the ferry leaves for the crossing to Ardvasar on the Isle of Skye.

Skye is a big, beautiful, mountainous island, and the turning point on this tour. If you have time to spare you may like to spend a day or two here, walking in the Cuillins or cycling up to Dunvegan in the north, or just resting before riding up to Kyleakin, for another brief ferry crossing to the Kyle of Lochalsh.

Once ashore, follow the A87 east into the Highlands, down the north shore of Loch Alsh and Loch Duich, into Glen Shiel and over a few high passes to Invergarry (50 miles) in Glen More, the Great Glen, that great cleft which divides the Highlands in two. Turn south here, on the A82, to Spean Bridge (16 miles) on the A86, past the memorial to World War II commandos who trained here, leaving Glen Spean to the east and going on to Fort William (10 miles). Built in the late seventeenth century to subdue the clans, it is now a tourist trap, but a good touring centre. The first trip from here is on the short road up to the foot of Ben Nevis, which at 4408 ft is Britain's highest mountain. Now start the last leg of this tour, south to the bridge at Ballachulish (12 miles), and then east into Glencoe for the steep climb up, past the ruined villages of the Macdonalds, on to the open bleakness of Rannoch Moor and across to Bridge of Orchy (26 miles). There is a very comfortable hotel at Bridge of Orchy, and from here a further 12 miles brings you to Crianlarich, on to the West Highland Line and the end of this tour.

TOUR 11

Across the North

The difference between landscape and landscape is small, but there is a great difference between the beholders.
RALPH WALDO EMERSON

Distance   236 miles

Time   One week

Counties   Cumbria, North Yorkshire, Humberside

Maps   GT No.6 (North England)
National Series No.34 (Lake District), No.35 (Darlington and North Yorkshire), No.36 (Teesside and Yorks Moors)

Guidebooks   *Portrait of Cumbria*, J. D. Marshall (Hale)
Portrait of Humberside, I. E. Broadhead (Hale)

Starting point   St Bees Head

Plotting this ride was a fascinating task, and since it worked in practice, it may prove the model for other rides when more obvious themes or reasons are lacking. The basic idea was to ride east to west across England as a counterweight to the popular ride from Land's End to John O' Groats. The extreme points chosen were St Bees Head in Cumbria and Flamborough Head in what is now Humberside. There was no particular reason for choosing these two points, but I drew a pencil line directly across the map and the tour described here charts the attempt to follow that line as closely as possible. Such resolves can get the tourist into some curious places. This is not a bad way to plan an off-beat tour since it eliminates the possibility of compromise – and incidentally calls for good map reading. The tour is highly varied and the route, running as it does over the Pennine spine of England, is rarely very flat. It can be ridden from either end, but west–east has the advantage of the prevailing wind and seems, to me at least, more natural, although getting to the start is something of a safari, for there are few convenient rail connections.

Accommodation is easy to find, and the roads, ranging from very

Rievaulx Abbey, North Yorkshire.

minor to the A class, are always good. In spring at least, this route will
never be too crowded.

St Bees Head in Cumbria lies north and west of St Bees itself, the
railway terminal for this tour. Walk, or ride, up to the headland and
begin with a look west, to the Isle of Man and out to Ireland, before
turning your face to the east.

From St Bees Head ride into Egremont (2 miles), followed by a long
run, first down the B5345 on to the A595 for 6 miles to Gosforth. Turn
east here to Santan Bridge and Eskdale Green. To the north lie the
high Fells, a good country for walkers, but the cyclist's road climbs
and climbs over the Hard Knott and Wrynose passes, with gradients
of 1 in 4 and 1 in 5, and so down to Ambleside (21 miles), a good first
stop after conquering some very high hills. As a glance at the map will
quickly reveal, most of the Lakeland roads run north–south, and
those which probe into the Fells soon peter out. The tour route lies to
the north, but Shap Fell and the other hills bar the way, so you must
skirt them to the south, 4 miles on the A591 to Windermere, then a
further 9 miles to Kendal. Leave Kendal on the A6, forking right after
a scant mile on to the A685 for Tebay (10 miles), and then, almost
parallel with my pencil line, to Coldbeck, over Ash Fell, right on to a

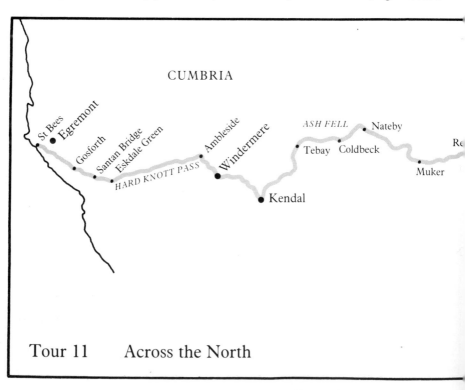

Tour 11   Across the North

minor road, then up to Nateby (12 miles), on the B6259.

From Nateby a marvellous, peaceful minor road, the B6270, runs east across the wild and open country of the Yorkshire Dales to Reeth (21 miles), 10 miles west of Richmond. At Reeth take the southern road, the B6270, following the Gill beck to Barden Moor and Appleton, crossing the A1 near Kirkby Fleetham (16 miles). From here it is a short ride on the A684 into Northallerton. This is one place bisected by the pencil line, but it stands at the western edge of the North York Moors, and the path across the moors towards Flamborough is again a crooked one. Find the minor road south to Crosby (5 miles), then over the A19, east to Cowesby (4 miles), a route then barred to the east by Hambleton Hill. To avoid it, go south to little Felixkirk, then north and east to Rievaulx (27 miles), and then a mile further into Helmsley.

Given that minor roads are more fun than main ones, drop south on to the B1257 at Sproxton, and follow this road all the way, south and east, into the market town of Malton (21 miles). Here the pencil line lies some miles to the north, but a good road runs almost due east, through Settington and Foxholes and passing a little to the north of Bridlington. Follow it right up to the finishing point of this tour on the North Sea at Flamborough Head (35 miles).

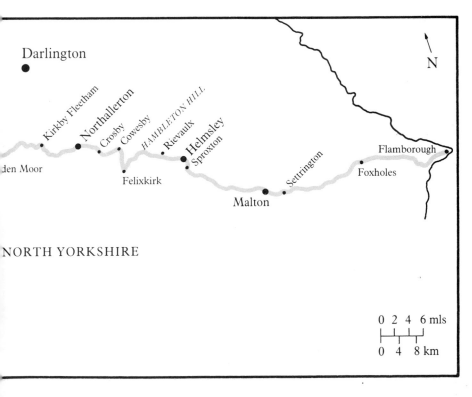

Hard Knott Pass, Cumbria.

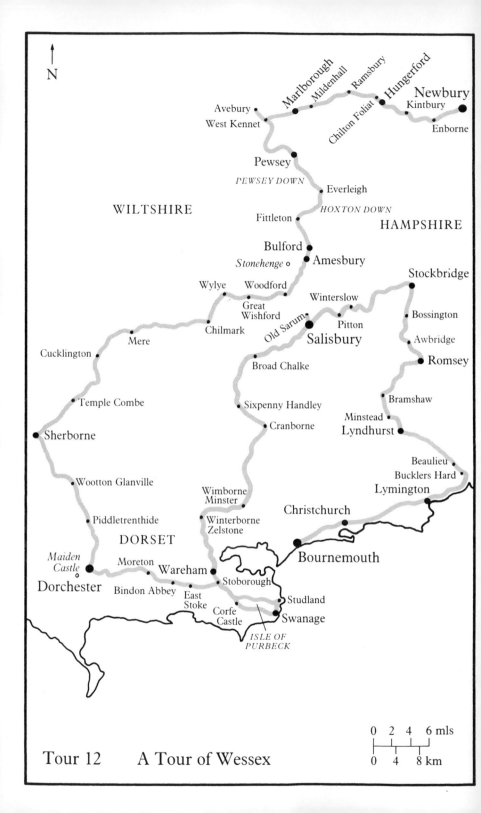

Tour 12   A Tour of Wessex

TOUR 12

A Tour of Wessex

She is full of famous towns, scarcely to be matched for beauty and ancientness in the rest of the world.
EDWARD HUTTON

Distance   360 miles

Time   One or two weeks

Counties   Wiltshire, Dorset, Hampshire

Maps   GT No.2 (South Coast)
National Series No.8 (Reading and Salisbury Plain), No.4 (Dorset), No.5 (Hampshire)

Guidebooks   *A View of Wessex*, G. N. Wright (Hale)
The Hampshire Village Book, Anthony Brode, (Countryside Books)
A Visitor's Guide to Somerset and Dorset, Alan Proctor (Moorland Publishing)

Starting point   Newbury

When people, especially from overseas, think of the English countryside, the place they imagine in the mind's eye closely resembles Wessex. Therefore I have to begin by pointing out that Wessex, as such, does not exist. The Saxon Kingdom of Wessex has not existed these thousand years or more, and the present 'Wessex' of popular imagination owes more to Thomas Hardy than to King Alfred – a place of leafy lanes, quiet streams, grey stone towns, sheep and sturdy peasants. Most of these, with the exception of the peasants, can be found in the counties of Hampshire, Dorset and Wiltshire, all of which feature to a greater or lesser degree in Hardy's Wessex, which is the area covered by this tour.

This is a highly varied part of Britain which offers a correspondingly rich tour. It begins with a glimpse of the Downs, tours the green Kennet Valley, strikes across the open spaces of Salisbury Plain, visits prehistoric Stonehenge and historic Stourhead, and then wanders east across Dorset and Hampshire, well supplied with those leafy lanes that cyclists like to roll down.

135

Newbury is a pleasant little town, but it need not delay you long. Find the minor road to the west, skirting the Kennet and Avon Canal and the railway, and follow it through Enborne and Kintbury to Hungerford (11 miles), a large village on the A4. From here pick up the B road beside the river Kennet for Chilton Foliat, one of those dreamlike little villages with thatched cottages and old-world inns. Follow the road west to Ramsbury on the Downs, through Mildenhall, and into Marlborough (13 miles). Formerly a coaching stage on the Bath Road, Marlborough has a wide main street still lined with coaching inns. At the western end lies Marlborough College, one of the great English public schools.

Leave Marlborough by the A4, a pleasant road much less crowded with heavy lorries since the M4 opened, so there is no real problem in covering the 8 miles west to Avebury. The village is surrounded by prehistoric standing stones or *menhirs*, arranged in rings. To the south-west lies the pudding-shaped mound of Silbury Hill, another prehistoric relic beside the A4. The countryside here is very beautiful, with sweeping views across open fields and downland, the crests crowned with tall beeches, the slopes often marked with white figures cut in the chalk. After looking round Avebury, return to the A4 and at West Kennet take a minor road south into the Vale of Pewsey, turning left at Alton Priors across the Kennet and Avon Canal again, noting the white horse on the hillside, to Pewsey itself (12 miles). One of the many English Avons flows by here: follow it south, but on minor roads, over Pewsey Down to the A342 (4 miles) east to Everleigh, then across Hoxton Down to Fittleton and south into Bulford and Amesbury (12 miles). This busy market town on the A303 lies a little to the east of the main attraction hereabouts, Stonehenge, a prehistoric stone circle and Druidic temple.

The site has been marred in recent years by carparks, walkways, signposts, fences and litter, but it still has to be seen. Afterwards ride back towards Amesbury, picking up the minor road to the river, then turn right or south along the river for Wilsford and Woodford (5 miles). Turn west here, resisting the temptation to continue south to Salisbury, which you will have an opportunity to visit later, and, crossing under the A36, head for Wylye (5 miles). Here you should ride west down the busy A303 for a mile south to Chilmark, then take the B3089 west for Mere and the great house at Stourhead, just to the north on the B3092 (18 miles).

Stourhead, in the village of Stourton, 3 miles north of Mere, is the heart of an estate village which now belongs to the National Trust. The time to see it is in late spring when the azaleas and rhododendrons are ablaze with colour, but it is lovely at any time of the year. The house was completed in 1724 and the river Stour was dammed to create the lake which complements it.

Incidentally, riding down here with a friend on another occasion, we thought to reduce the distance by riding through the lion park at Longleat, a little to the north. Fortunately we were stopped by a keeper, who suggested that the lions might regard us as meals on wheels! We took his point.

From Stourhead, return to Mere and turn west down the A303 for 3 miles, then turn south for Cucklington, working south and west on minor roads to the little town of Sherborne (17 miles). Sherborne School, founded in 1550, took over many of the medieval buildings in what had been a monastic centre since the eighth century. Do not leave before visiting Half Moon Street, full of fine buildings, and Sherborne Abbey church, one of the finest medieval churches in the south, where two Saxon kings lie buried. Sherborne Castle – or rather the New Castle – dating from 1590, was briefly the home of Sir Walter Raleigh.

You are now entering the heart of the Hardy country, with a 20-mile ride due south to the old county town of Dorchester. Leave Sherborne by the A352, turning on to the B3146 after 5 miles and heading south into the land of the Piddles and the Puddles. The Piddles are two small villages along the B3143, Piddletrenthide and Piddlehinton, where those to whom such things appeal can buy bottles of Piddlewater. The Puddles, Affpuddle, Tolpuddle, Puddletown and several more, lie to the east. On the way down the river, turn west for an 8-mile diversion to see the Cerne Abbas Giant, a phallic figure carved in the chalk hillside.

The cyclist's path follows the course of the Piddle (or Trent, if you prefer), then turns off on the B3143 for Dorchester, Hardy's Casterbridge (10 miles). Mostly a Georgian town, it stands on an old site, for the Romans had a camp here. Judge Jeffreys held one of his Bloody Assizes in Dorchester after the Monmouth Rebellion of 1685, and the Tolpuddle Martyrs were tried here in 1834, for the 'crime' of association, or attempting to form a trade union, and later transported to Australia. A little to the south lies Maiden Castle, an Iron Age hill fort stormed by the Romans in AD 43. The museum in Dorchester contains some excellent relics of this ancient siege. Hardy lived at

Lower Bockhampton, 3 miles to the east, and his house can be visited.

At Dorchester I felt torn between the desire to head west to Lyme Regis and the need to turn east and complete a logical tour, besides sticking to my plan. Needs had to prevail, so leave by the A352 for Wareham, turning off left after a mile to pick up a series of minor roads through Moreton, across the A352 at Bindon Abbey to East Stoke and Stoborough (18 miles), on the Isle of Purbeck, claimed by many, to be the most beautiful part of Dorset.

Turn south and circle the island to Corfe Castle, a spectacle in itself. Continue to Swanage, a seaside resort, north to Studland, a very beautiful village set in the heathlands of Wareham Moor, and then back down the B3351 to Wareham (22 miles).

This is a good place to stop and rest for a day, close to the sea, full of old inns, with the yacht-dotted expanse of Poole Harbour to the east and the Isle of Purbeck shimmering to the south. Next day, avoiding Poole and Bournemouth, ride up the A351 to where the B3075 turns north, and follow this for 6 miles before turning east on the A31, south of Winterbourne Zelstone, for Wimborne Minster (8 miles). One of the finest churches in Dorset, it is mainly Norman and built of red and white stone; it contains marvellous tombs, choir stalls and a wooden medieval figure on the bell tower called Quarter Jack. From here head north towards the beautiful woods of Cranborne Chase, first up the B3078 to Cranborne (10 miles), then along the B3081 to Sixpenny Handley at the foot of the Chase (4 miles), then to Broad Chalke and east into the cathedral city of Salisbury (15 miles).

A beautiful, ancient town, Salisbury is full of medieval houses, old inns, bookshops and broad, tree-lined lawns. Salisbury Cathedral was built relatively quickly, between 1120 and 1258, so it is a pure example of Early English Gothic, although the 404-ft needle spire was added later, in 1334. The interior is full of interesting things to see, including the oldest clock in England, still in working order, installed here in 1386. Spare a day for Salisbury, and take a look at Old Sarum, 2 miles to the north, before departing for Stockbridge.

Leave on the busy A30, turning off right for Pitton after 3 miles, and working your way east on minor roads, returning to the A30 for the last 3 miles to Stockbridge (15 miles). Stockbridge, a market town and once a coaching centre, lies in the valley of the river Test, one of

OPPOSITE ABOVE Ashmore, Dorset
BELOW Salisbury Cathedral

Village of Corfe Castle, Dorset.

the finest trout streams in Britain. From here follow the Test south to Romsey (10 miles), a fine little town; Romsey Abbey is the ancestral home of the Mountbattens. Then weave a path on minor roads, steering around Southampton, through Bramshaw and Brook to Lyndhurst (15 miles) in the New Forest.

Near Brook stands the Rufus Stone, marking the spot where William Rufus, son of the Conqueror, was killed while out hunting. Lyndhurst lies in open country in the heart of the Forest, and from here the B3056 leads to Beaulieu (7 miles), with its huge motor museum and old abbey, the home of Lord Montagu. Close by lies Bucklers Hard, once a famous shipyard and now a sailing centre. Many of the ships of Nelson's navy were built here and there is a maritime museum. From here ride south and pick up the road for Lymington, another sailing centre on the Solent, before turning west to New Milton and so into Bournemouth (18 miles) and the end of this long and fascinating journey across a part of England that does, indeed, seem very like the Wessex that Hardy knew and immortalized.

TOUR 13

A Tour Along the South Coast – Dover to Plymouth

Oh happy Britain, wherein are woods without wild beasts and fields without noysom serpents; but infinite numbers of milch cattel and sheep weighed down with rich fleeces; and, that which is most comfortable, long days and lightsome nights.
A ROMAN CHRONICLER

Distance   456 miles

Time   Two weeks

Counties   Kent, East Sussex, West Sussex, Hampshire, Dorset, Devon

Maps   GT No.2 (South Coast)
National Series No.10 (Kent), No.6 (Sussex), No.5 (New Forest), No.4 (Dorset), No.2 (South Devon)

Guidebooks   *South Coast Landscapes*, Jo Darke (Batsford)

Starting point   Dover

This tour was suggested by a French friend of mine, a keen cyclist and the purser on a cross-Channel ferry, who told me of his dream to get off at Plymouth, ride to Dover, cross over to France and ride home again to Roscoff in Brittany, a coastal tour in two countries; did I know any good routes? At the time I didn't, but this tour is the result of his question. The big problem lies in the fact that the south coast is very well developed, and riding through one set of traffic lights after another, to be blocked at every turn by one-way streets, is not a very good way to spend a holiday. Planning this tour took a long time, but, as is usually the case, the more time you put into planning, the more fun you will have on the ride.

This tour reverses the direction I was asked about. It runs through the coastal counties of England from Kent to Devon, staying as close to the sea as possible while avoiding towns and traffic-jammed main roads wherever possible – unfortunately it isn't always possible.

This is a journey for late spring and early summer, or indeed any

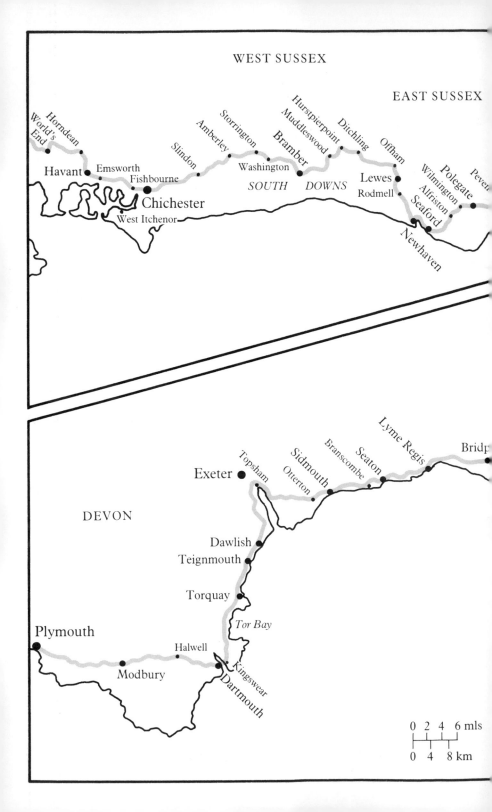

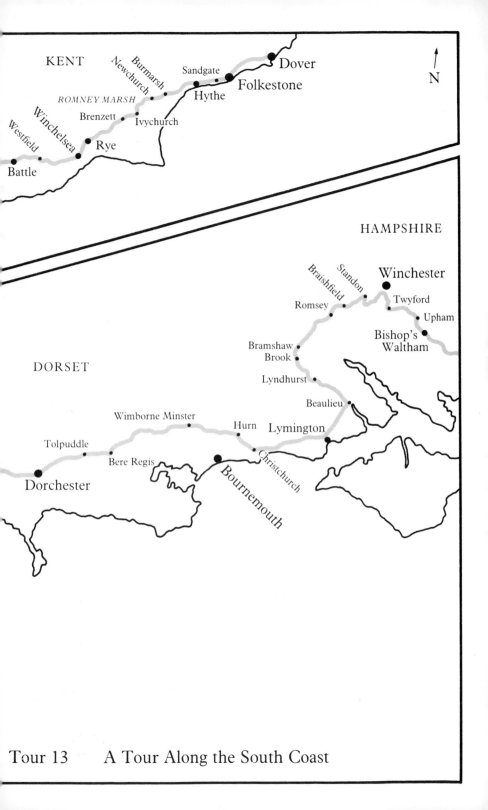

KENT

Dover

Burmarsh

Newchurch

Sandgate

Folkestone

ROMNEY MARSH

Hythe

Brenzett

Ivychurch

Westfield

Winchelsea

Rye

Battle

N

HAMPSHIRE

Standon

Braishfield

Winchester

Romsey

Twyford

Upham

Bramshaw

Bishop's
Waltham

Brook

DORSET

Lyndhurst

Beaulieu

Wimborne Minster

Hurn

Lymington

Tolpuddle

Christchurch

Bere Regis

Bournemouth

Dorchester

Tour 13   A Tour Along the South Coast

Oast houses near Headcorn in Kent.

time outside the holiday months of July and August. The terrain is fairly gentle, except for the South Downs, and there is plenty of accommodation. I found it best to start looking about for a good bed and breakfast at around 4 pm, with pubs to fall back on after opening time if all else failed.

The tour is a long one, and if you want to have time for sightseeing, aim to ride between 40 and 50 miles each day.

I nearly gave up in Dover. The one-way traffic system must have been designed by the man who invented the Rubic cube. After half an hour wandering about I gave up and walked along the footpath up the steep hill to the castle. I don't know where the footpath begins, for I found it by accident, so you must use your initiative. That said, Dover has some good sights, notably the splendid Norman castle with its Roman lighthouse, set high on the white cliffs and besieged by the French in the Barons' War. The way out lies past Dover Priory Station and into the lorry-laden A20 Folkestone road, but turn off on the outskirts into a minor road for Folkestone (7 miles), which can be swiftly crossed for Sandgate and Hythe (5 miles), where I arrived in a slightly better temper.

Hythe lies at the eastern end of Romney Marsh, a blissfully empty region. Take the minor roads across, past Newchurch and Ivychurch, both of which are worth a look as are all the churches on the Marsh, to Brenzett (12 miles) on the B2080. From here take the A259 for 7 miles, a quick dash into the little town of Rye, a splendid place to end the first day of the tour. Next morning stroll about the cobbled streets of this old Cinque Port – it was formerly on the coast, but the sea has retreated, leaving it as a kind of island rising out of the low-lying marshland. The Cinque Ports were actually seven medieval towns, which gained privileges and charters from the king in return for supplying ships to the navy. Rye produced generations of seamen and pirates, who raided the French coast and were raided in their turn. The old town was destroyed in 1337, and the famous Mermaid Inn, dating from 1420, is a relic of the 'new' town.

Winchelsea, 5 miles to the west, is another stranded Cinque Port. It was laid out as a *bastide*, or fortified town, by Edward I, and once had a population of 6000, ten times that of today. The Court Hall Museum tells the story of the Cinque Ports.

Leave Winchelsea on the A251, then take minor roads through Westfield Moor for the small town of Battle (11 miles), where in 1066, the one date every Englishman remembers, William of Normandy defeated the Saxon Harold. The Normans called the battle Senlac, but history has donated the glory to Hastings, yet another Cinque Port, which lies 6 miles to the south. William endowed Battle Abbey to commemorate his victory, and the high altar is said to stand on the spot where Harold fell. The buildings were ravaged at the Reformation and are still mostly in ruins, except for the gatehouse and the Abbot's Hall, which is now a girls' school. The battlefield itself is much as it was, and the museum has excellent maps, and a reproduction of the Bayeux Tapestry.

Leave Battle on the B2095 and go south and west on to the A27 for Pevensey, where William landed, and so to Polegate (16 miles). Ride west to Wilmington, which lies on the north side of the South Downs

The Dorset coast near Lulworth.

and is overlooked by a tall hill figure carved in the chalk, known as the Long Man of Wilmingdon, and down the B2108 to Seaford. The South Downs are quite hilly, and you will stay with them across Sussex and into Hampshire, with the B2108 serving as an introduction.

Follow the A259 to Newhaven (15 miles), then take the minor road to Lewes (7 miles), a fine old town on the river, before riding north, past the site of the battle of 1264 in which Simon de Montfort beat Henry III in the Barons' War. Turn at Offham, which has a fine church, for a ride across the Downs to Ditchling Beacon (6 miles). The run down from the Beacon to Ditchling village is well known to those thousands of cyclists who slog up the hill every year on the London to Brighton Bike Ride. From Ditchling the route weaves across Sussex through a host of pretty places, to Hurstpierpoint, Hassocks, west on the A281, then south on the A2037 to Bramber, then to Steyning. From here the road still lies north of the Downs, with the tall clump of beach trees that marks the ancient Chanctonbury Ring up above, to Washington (21 miles).

Cross the A24 here and after 2 miles turn south at Storrington on to the B2139 to Amberley, Slindon and, with another brave dash down the A27, into the cathedral city of Chichester (8 miles). Allow a good long day for the journey from Lewes to Chichester by this winding, but always interesting route.

Chichester lies at the eastern end of its harbour, a vast estuary fringed by delightful villages, and in order to see some of them, and Chichester itself, stay two nights here and devote a full day to local exploration. In Chichester the cathedral is a must, and the well-known theatre is worth an evening visit. Attractive places round about include Bosham, where King Canute is said to have asked the tide to stop; Dell Quay, which has a fine pub at the head of the estuary; West Itchenor, a sailing centre; Fishbourne, for the Roman villa . . . the list is endless. After a full day (or two) leave on the B2178 through Emsworth for Westbourne and Havant (10 miles). From Havant you can ride into Portsmouth to see Nelson's flagship, HMS *Victory*, but otherwise it's just another big busy town, so skirt Havant on the B2149 for Horndean (15 miles) and take the minor road west through World's End to the Meon Valley (10 miles).

You will need to skirt Southampton Water, so the route turns north to Bishops Waltham, Upham and Twyford (12 miles). Here it would be sensible to make a diversion to see Winchester, another fine, historic city, and leave there on the A3090 to Standon, then to Braishfield and into Romsey, where this tour follows Tour 12 for some 35 miles as far as Christchurch on the outskirts of Bournemouth (see page 140).

At Christchurch, pick up the B3073 past the airport at Hurn, to Wimborne Minster (12 miles), where you can either follow the path of Route 12 to Dorchester, or do as I did and blitz down the A31 and A35 for 25 miles through Bere Regis and the 'Puddles' to Thomas Hardy's Casterbridge – Dorchester, a very beautiful Georgian town.

The main roads here are wide and not too crowded, so follow the A35 again, or in high summer take the quiet road just to the north, for a rolling ride to Bridport (15 miles), another Georgian town, which acquired its fame and fortune by making ropes for the Royal Navy (and the hangman). The wide streets were designed as ropewalks. A further 10 miles brings you to Lyme Regis, a charming, unspoilt seaside town which has featured in literature, from Jane Austen's *Persuasion* to John Fowles's *The French Lieutenant's Woman*, and is full of history. Edward I gave it the 'Regis' suffix, and the Duke of Monmouth landed here in 1685 to start his rebellion against James II. The Cobb, a medieval breakwater, is curious and impressive. I like Lyme; it's a place to linger in. Afterwards cross the border and enter Devon, the red-earth county.

Staying close to the coast this tour passes on to Seaton, Brancombe and Sidmouth (16 miles), all attractive places. From Sidmouth a minor road runs to Otterton; on the B3179, over the gorse and pine trees of Woodbury Common, you can cycle down to Topsham on the river Exe and so into Exeter (15 miles). Stay to see the cathedral and the famous Ship Museum before setting out on the last stage of this coastal ride, down to Dawlish and Teignmouth (16 miles), a splendid route with first the wide estuary and then the open sea lying on your left. From Teignmouth it is only 8 miles to the elegant resort of Torquay. There is a great ride from Torquay round Tor Bay to the fishing port of Brixham (15 miles); then a minor road, the B3205, leads to Kingswear (5 miles), where a ferry takes travellers across the river Dart into beautiful Dartmouth, the home of the Royal Naval College. There are two great castles, one on each headland, many yachts and some fine Elizabethan houses on the quay. From here the cyclist's road, the B3207, leads due west to Modbury (17 miles), and then over the last 12 miles into Plymouth where, up on the windy Hoe, overlooking the harbour, you will end this journey.

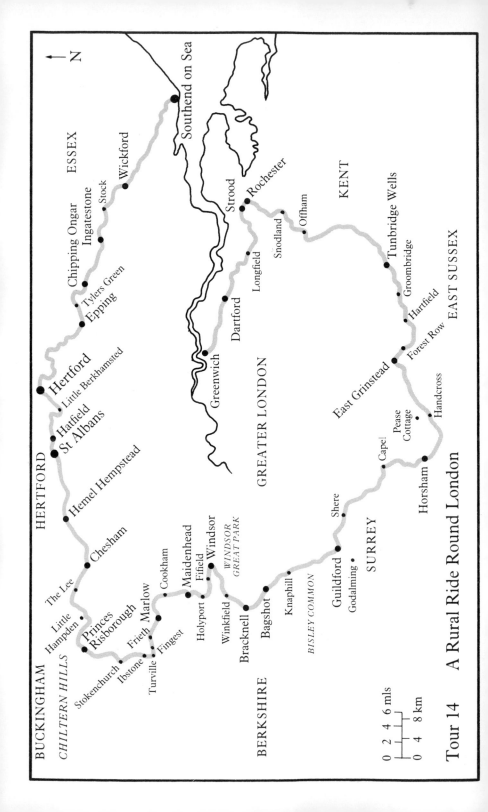

N

BUCKINGHAM

ESSEX

CHILTERN HILLS

Southend on Sea

Wickford

Chipping Ongar
Ingatestone
Stock

Tylers Green
Epping

HERTFORD

Hertford
Little Berkhamsted

Hatfield
St Albans

Hemel Hempstead

Strood
Rochester

KENT

Snodland
Offham

Longfield

Dartford

Tunbridge Wells

Groombridge

Hartfield

Forest Row

EAST SUSSEX

Greenwich

GREATER LONDON

East Grinstead

Chesham

The Lee

Little
Hampden

Cookham

Maidenhead
Fifield
Windsor

*WINDSOR
GREAT PARK*

Handcross

Capel

Pease
Cottage

Marlow

Princes
Risborough

Frieth

Holyport

Winkfield

Shere

Stokenchurch

Ibstone

Turville Fingest

Bracknell

Bagshot

Knaphill

BISLEY COMMON

Guildford

Godalming

SURREY

Horsham

BERKSHIRE

0   2   4   6 mls

0   4   8 km

Tour 14   A Rural Ride Round London

TOUR 14

A Rurual Ride Round London

London is a splendid place to live in for those that can get out of it.
LORD BALFOUR, *The Observer, 1944*

Distance 340 miles

Time One to two weeks

Counties Kent, Surrey, West Sussex, Berkshire, Buckinghamshire, Hertfordshire, Essex

Maps GT No.2 (South Coast), No.5 (East Anglia)
National Series No.9 (London and Surrey), No.10 (Kent), No.8 (Reading), No.14 (Oxford), No.15 (Hertfordshire and Buckinghamshire), No. 16 (Essex)

Guidebooks *South-East England and East Anglia*, Roger Higham (Ward Lock)

Starting point Greenwich Palace, south-east London

London is full of cyclists, all with cycle-touring potential, and most cycle tourists visiting Britain will want to spend some time there, if only to see the sights. It is also a very good central point in which to pause for a while, and to get organized for any of the tours in this book, so for those and other reasons it seemed logical to include a tour around London, visiting some of the attractive and historic places which lie just beyond the central conurbation.

As rides go, it is not particularly long, and the terrain is gentle, but there are two big problems: traffic and road signs. There are so many roads that it is quite easy to get lost, and I therefore advise riders not to worry about precise route finding in the Greater London area, but to head in the general direction of the next point worth visiting – this will, in the end, lead them to it. The terrain is generally flat, or at the most, gently rolling. Accommodation can also be a problem in summer, for though there is plenty of it the prices can be very high, forcing you further out into the country searching for pubs or good bed and breakfasts.

The countryside around London is full of pretty places, so allow yourself time to see them. This is a great ride for the spring and

151

autumn, before the traffic builds up in the height of summer. That apart, it's fun to pick one's way slowly on small roads round a great city, although not everyone I met seemed to think so. I asked one taxi driver for directions and, when he found out what I was doing, he looked me up and down slowly and said, 'You must be bloody mad.' Mad or not, this tour begins by Greenwich Palace in south-east London, a marvellous departure point.

At Greenwich, chain up your cycle by the east gate and ask one of the gatekeepers to keep an eye on it while you visit the Maritime Museum. I left my panniers at the coat-and-bag counter, where they had to be searched, but it would be a shame to leave historic Greenwich without visiting the Maritime Museum, the Royal Observatory up on the hill, which marks the Zero Meridian, or that romantic clipper ship, the *Cutty Sark*, and Francis Chichester's *Gipsy Moth IV*, not to mention some of the local pubs.

Then ride up the steep hill to Blackheath, which preserves the atmosphere of a picturesque village, and head south-east down the A2 towards Rochester. Turn off on to the B270 at Dartford (12 miles), past the Roman villa, and take the B260 and B2009 to Strood and Rochester on the river Medway (25 miles), following the road which Chaucer's pilgrims took to Canterbury (see Tour 2). Rochester Castle is well worth a look before taking the A228 south towards West Malling (8 miles). You should veer west at Snodland to Offham and pick up a good minor road, the B2106, which with the B2015 leads down to the spa town of Tunbridge Wells (15 miles). Much of this ride is now through attractive countryside, with the city left far behind. Tunbridge Wells is an attractive town, the Bath of the eastern counties, famous for the Pantiles, a line of elegant eighteenth- and early ninteenth-century houses and shops with a once-tiled walk which leads down to the mineral springs.

From here the route runs west to Groombridge and Hartfield, first on the A264, then on the B2110, through Forest Row into East Grinstead (17 miles). West of here lies the M23 and Gatwick Airport which have to be skirted to the south, still on the B2110 to Handcross, then up the A23 to the oddly named village of Pease Pottage and into the market town of Horsham (20 miles).

OPPOSITE The Woods on Box Hill, on the North Downs.

OVERLEAF Epping Forest.

To avoid the A24, take the minor road north towards Capel (8 miles), and here turn west on the B2126 for Shere, past the beautiful village of Abinger Hammer, and into Guildford, the county town (20 miles). Five miles away to the south, and therefore too close to miss visiting, lies Godalming, the home of the Cyclists' Touring Club. This Surrey countryside is quite hilly in places, though every hill gives fine and rewarding views, and it is full of good pubs.

Returning to Guildford, take the A322 north past Pirbright and the rifle ranges at Bisley to Bagshot, and then on, between high rhododendrons and gorse bushes ablaze with colour in the summer, across Bagshot Common to Bracknell (17 miles). From here ride into Windsor (8 miles), through the pretty village of Winkfield and Windsor Forest. Windsor is well worth a day's rest to see the castle and wander in the streets of the town, and visit Eton, site of the famous public school, just across the river. Then take the minor road along the river for a little while, past the racecourse to Fifield and Holyport, an attractive hamlet which leads to Maidenhead (6 miles).

Maidenhead is a busy, much modernized town, but the riverside is very beautiful, so follow the A4094 past Boulter's Lock to Cookham (2 miles). Stop here to see the museum devoted to the artist Stanley Spencer, who lived here, and the beautiful riverside church, and then ride up the very steep hill to Cliveden (2 miles), the former home of the Astors now owned by the National Trust.

From here it is a level 5 miles into Marlow, a very attractive Thames-side town with Georgian houses lining the High Street. A good minor road leads from Marlow into the Chiltern hills, through Frieth, Fingest, Turville and Ibstone to Stokenchurch (7 miles). All these Chiltern villages are attractive, but Turville and Fingest are exquisite, and should not be missed. They look marvellous in the spring when the blossom is out, and in autumn when the beech leaves have changed to rich colours.

Stokenchurch lies on the very top of the Chiltern escarpment, and the cycle route follows minor roads down the western wall to the little town of Princes Risborough (8 miles), an up-and-down ride through the Chiltern beech woods, before turning east, through Little Hampden and The Lee, still on narrow Chiltern roads, into Chesham in the heart of the Chiltern Hundreds (15 miles). The Stewardship of the Chiltern Hundreds was once an onerous position, for the Steward had to catch and hang the highwaymen and footpads who lived in the Chiltern Woods and robbed travellers on the Oxford road. As an office of profit under the Crown it cannot be held by a Member of Parliament, so even today any Member who wishes to resign his seat – or has to – applies for the Stewardship of the Chiltern Hundreds, and is therefore allowed to resign his position.

From Chesham take the B4505, which climbs steeply up from the Chess Valley, and then descends into Hemel Hempstead (7 miles) before turning east to St Albans (6 miles). A greatly underrated place, it contains the splendid cathedral of England's first martyr, St Alban, and the remains of the Roman city of Verulamium, which was destroyed by Boudicca, the warrior queen. Allow a night stop here and visit the old parts of the city by the river Ver.

Heading east now, across Hertfordshire, take the B158 into Hertford. Then weave across country to Epping (23 miles), and then cutting a little to the north up the B181 to Tylers Green and into Chipping Ongar (6 miles).

From Ongar, the cyclist's roads run east across Essex to that playground of East End Londoners, Southend-on-Sea (37 miles). If the main roads can be avoided the countryside is fairly flat and very pleasant, so choose the minor, unmarked roads through Ingatestone, Stock and Wickford, which will bring you to the end of Southend pier and the end of this journey. From here it is best to take a train back to London; all the Thames crossing points are barred to cyclists until well upstream, and the ride through the suburbs is unattractive.

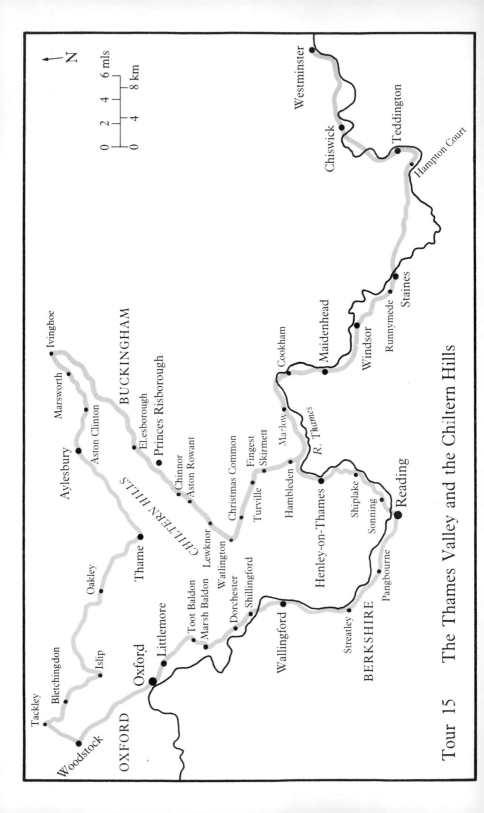

Tour 15   The Thames Valley and the Chiltern Hills

TOUR 15

The Thames Valley and the Chiltern Hills

The valleys of England are too many and too fair, from the fairest of all through which the Thames flows seaward.
EDWARD HUTTON

Distance   186 miles

Time   One week

Counties   Middlesex, Berkshire, Oxfordshire

Maps   GT No.2 (South Coast), No.4 (Midlands)
National Series No.9 (London and Surrey), No.8 (Reading and Salisbury), No.14 (Oxford)

Guidebooks   *Portrait of the Chilterns*, Elizabeth Cull (Hale)
A Visitor's Guide to the Chilterns, Neil Lands (Moorland Publishing)
The Thames Valley Heritage Walk, Miles Jebb (Constable)

Starting point   Westminster

This tour takes you through two different but attractive areas of England, and begins by following the course of the river Thames from the Palace of Westminster to the town of Woodstock in Oxfordshire. Having got there, you have to get back, and the return journey takes a wide swing through the Chiltern Hills, which are very close to London and yet virtually unknown to Londoners. The route will appeal to lovers of English history, for it passes some famous places: those who enjoy visiting palaces and stately homes will have the ride of their lives. That apart, I have chosen roads which are well off the tourist track, and those who like quiet English villages will not be disappointed either. This tour has something for everyone. This is not a long tour, for even with diversions it cannot exceed 200 miles, but allow a full week because a lot of time will be spent sightseeing.

I recommend you to ride this route in the spring or early autumn before the summer traffic builds up. The terrain is fairly gentle, if a trifle steep here and there in the Chilterns, and there is plenty of accommodation outside the high season. The tour begins outside the Houses of Parliament.

Ride west from the Houses of Parliament down the Victoria Embankment, up to Earls Court and then out along the Great West Road, turning off at Chiswick (2 miles) for a visit first to Kew Gardens and then to Syon House, which also has beautiful gardens (5 miles). Then follow the road signs through a maze of a streets to Teddington (5 miles), where a lock and weir mark the point where the Thames becomes tidal, and on to Hampton Court (3 miles) to see the great Tudor palace built by Cardinal Wolsey and taken over by Henry VIII. Then take the A308 along the river to Staines (11 miles) and Runnymede (2 miles) where, in 1215, the barons forced King John to accept the terms of Magna Carta. Close by, garden lovers will find the Savill Garden, beautiful in spring; on the hill above the river you can see the Royal Air Force Memorial. The worst of the traffic will now be behind you.

Six miles east of Staines lies Windsor, and Windsor Castle, best viewed from the Long Walk junction on the A308. Ride into Windsor for your first night stop, and allow at least half a day to visit the town, castle and Eton College, before leaving, still on the A308, for Maidenhead. Then take the A4094 beside the river, past Boulters Lock, to Cookham (9 miles) and the museum containing works by the artist Stanley Spencer. A very pretty riverside village, it has a fine church and a very old pub, the Bel and Dragon. Cross the river bridge and ride on for 4 miles into Marlow, which has Georgian houses in the High Street, a fine suspension bridge and a famous hotel by the river, the Compleat Angler. Pick up the A4155, a quiet road, and head for Henley-on-Thames (8 miles); at Hambleden a fine clapboard water mill, now converted into apartments, is well worth seeing.

Henley-on-Thames is busy during the first week of July when the Royal Regatta is held, but is otherwise a quaint attractive town with pleasant houses and restaurants. The Little Angel on the far side of the bridge is a very popular pub and restaurant. From Henley the A4155 follows the river through Shiplake to Reading (7 miles), but cyclists are advised to divert through the beautiful little village of Sonning, then up to the A4 and down the hill into Reading centre.

Whatever charm Reading once possessed it has long since lost. Leave by the A329 for Pangbourne, heading for Oxford along the

ABOVE Hambleden Mill, by the Thames near Henley. BELOW The village of Turville in the Chilterns.

river, but take your time, for this is a beautiful ride, past a host of pleasant places – Moulsford, South Stoke, through Goring and its twin village, Streatley, to historic Wallingford (15 miles). Cross the river for Shillingford and then ride up to Dorchester-on-Thames (4 miles), where you should visit the abbey. From here the A427 runs directly into Oxford, but the cycle route lies off this main road through two strangely named villages, March Baldon and Toot Baldon, on to the B480 and into Oxford via Littlemore (12 miles).

To know Oxford can take a lifetime, but do give it a full day. Stroll about on foot before leaving on the short ride to the turning point at Woodstock (8 miles), with diversions to see the Trout Inn at Godstow, and Sir Winston Churchill's grave at Bladon. That, with a tour of Blenheim Palace at Woodstock, will take another full day.

From Woodstock, take the minor road off the High Street for Tackley, a pretty Cotswold village, and then find the B4027 for Bletchingdon and Islip (10 miles), where the route turns across the curious chequerboard country of remote Otmoor, through Charlton and Murcot to Oakley, on to the B4011 for Thame (15 miles). Turn north-east at Thame and follow the A418 to Aylesbury (10 miles). The centre is still attractive, with a fine statue of John Hampden, the Parliamentarian soldier and a local squire, but it need not delay you long. Take the A41 past the Bell Inn at Aston Clinton and ride north, under the looming Chiltern escarpment to the east, past Marsworth and Pitstone windmill and into Ivinghoe (10 miles).

Ivinghoe Beacon marks the start of the long-distance walk called the Ridgeway Path. The cycle route follows the old road below the escarpment, the Icknield Way, south and west, along the B488 and A4011 to Ellesborough, which has a fine church, and then continues on the B4009, through the Kimbles, Chinnor, Aston Rowant and Lewknor into Watlington (23 miles), all of which are worth a pause. This ride, too, will probably occupy most of the day.

Turn in Watlington and ride up the steep hill to Christmas Common, on the top of the escarpment, which offers a marvellous view over the sweep of the Oxfordshire plain. Then drop down a very narrow road through the Chiltern beech woods to pretty Turville, overlooked by a windmill, then into Fingest with its ancient Saxon church and, through Skirmett, down to the Thames again at Hambleden Mill. From here it is only a few miles to either Marlow or Henley, both of which have railways stations, and in an hour or less you will be back in London.

162

TOUR 16

The West Country

But westward look, the land is bright.
A. H. CLOUGH, *Say Not the Struggle Naught Availeth*

Distance   580 miles

Time   Two to three weeks

Counties   Avon, Somerset, Devon, Cornwall

Maps   GT No.1 (West Country)
National Series No.1 (Cornwall), No.2 (South Devon), No.3 (North Devon), No.4 (Dorset), No.7 (Bristol and North Somerset)

Guidebooks   *Devon & Cornwall*, Denys Kay-Robinson (Bartholomew)
Moorland Visitors' Guide Series: *Devon*; *Cornwall*; *Somerset*

Starting point   Bristol

The West Country is a wonderful area for cycle touring. During the summer it is also a popular holiday region and the two are not always compatible, but fortunately tourism is restricted to a few months of the year in certain areas, and the West Country is a big place, full of minor roads. This tour, from Bristol down to Land's End and back, takes in most of the well-known places but gets off the beaten track as often as possible, and as always uses minor roads. The distance covered will depend very much on how much wandering you do, and how often you get lost, which is easy to do in the narrow West Country lanes.

The weather is usually milder than elsewhere in Britain, so the only snag for cyclists is the prevailing westerly winds which can blow head-on during the first leg of the tour, but give a useful boost on the return trip to the east. The terrain is varied but tends to be hilly, especially in North Devon and Cornwall, so getting a little fitter before the start would be a very good idea. Plenty of accommodation is available, although the main resorts tend to be full in July and August, and some hotels are closed at other times. Small parties of cyclists will

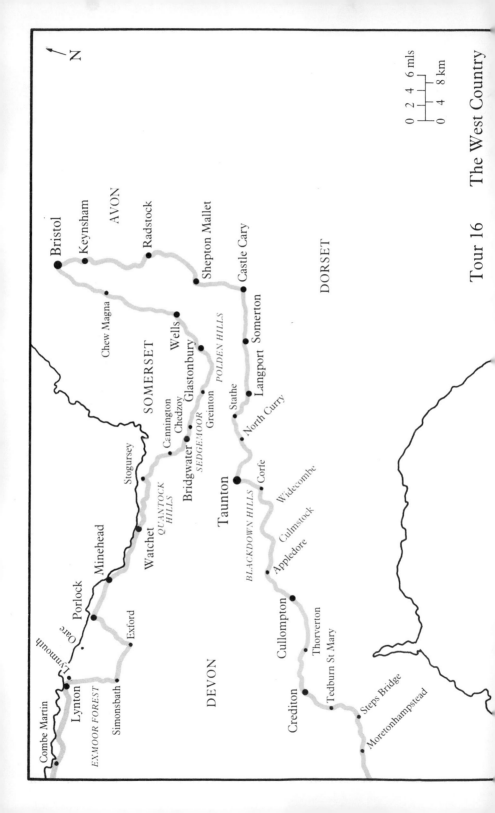

N

Combe Martin
Lynmouth
Lynton
Porlock
Oare
EXMOOR FOREST
Simonsbath
Exford
Minehead
Watchet
Stogursey
QUANTOCK HILLS
Cannington
Chedzoy
Bridgwater
SEDGEMOOR
Greinton
Stathe
North Curry
Corfe
Widecombe
Culmstock
Appledore
BLACKDOWN HILLS
Taunton
Cullompton
Thorverton
Tedburn St Mary
Crediton
Steps Bridge
Moretonhampstead

DEVON

Bristol
Keynsham
AVON
Radstock
Chew Magna
SOMERSET
Wells
Glastonbury
POLDEN HILLS
Shepton Mallet
Castle Cary
Somerton
Langport

DORSET

0 2 4 6 mls
0   4   8 km

Tour 16   The West Country

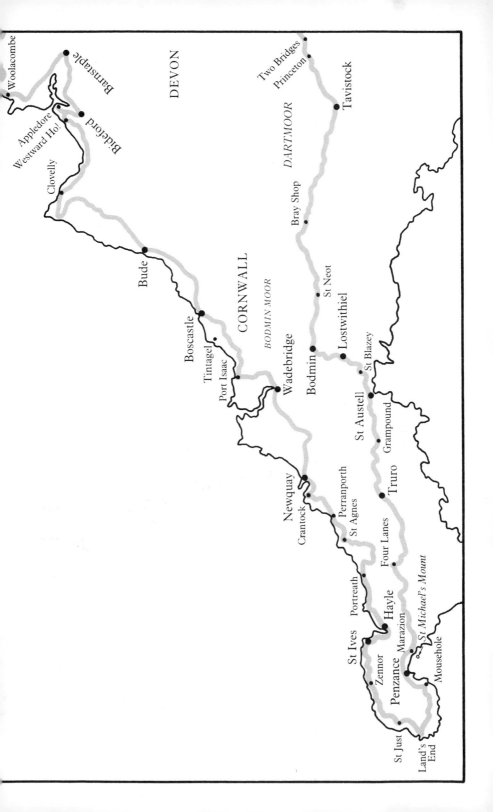

have no trouble finding somewhere to stay, and there are plenty of camp sites in the caves along the coast. Many of these are Camping Club sites, so a *carnet* or membership card might be useful.

Bristol is an interesting, lively, agreeable city, the capital of the west. A university town, it is also famous for the works of the engineer Isambard Kingdom Brunel, who built the Clifton Bridge, the Great Western Railway and the steamship *Great Britain*, which, now restored, is exhibited in the harbour.

When you leave, take the A38 for the south, turning left at Bishopsworth on to the B3114 for Chew Magna (8 miles), heading due south for your first stop, the cathedral city of Wells (23 miles). The antiquary John Leland said that Chew Magna 'Is a praty towne with a faire church', and 'praty' it is. A former wool town, it has a magnificent church full of memorial brasses, with a fine medieval effigy. The house next door, Chew Court, once belonged to the Bishop of Bath and Wells.

Wells itself is tiny, but the cathedral, which has medieval sculptures on the west front and a famous clock on which knights tilt every hour, on the hour, is magnificent. So too is the moated Bishop's Palace, just across the green; the swans which float on the moat about the Palace ring a bell at feeding time. It is one of those marvellous places where time has apparently stood still. Dragging yourself away from Wells, take the A39 to the next stop, the curious town of Glastonbury (5 miles), a pilgrim centre since Christianity first arrived in Britain.

According to legend King Arthur may be buried here, and the story goes that Joseph of Arimathea came to Glastonbury Tor to bury the chalice – the Holy Grail – which Christ used at the Last Supper. He planted his staff in the earth and it took root and flowered at Christmas, becoming known as the Glastonbury Thorn. See the ruined abbey, walk up to the tor, and visit the George Inn where medieval pilgrims stayed, and St John's church, before leaving to ride across the north of Sedgemoor, site in 1685 of the last battle fought on English soil. Take the A361 to Greinton across the Polden Hills, then the minor road to Chedzoy and so into Bridgwater (12 miles).

The Sedgemoor Inn in Bridgwater exhibits relics of the battle, but Bridgwater is in any case an old town, a former port full of interesting

Church steps, Minehead.

buildings. Fine views over Sedgemoor can be had from the tower of St Mary's, from which the ill-fated Duke of Monmouth saw his army defeated. Leave Bridgwater on the A39, turning off after 4 miles at Cannington, on to a minor road that leads to Stogursey, with the Quantock Hills looming to the south-west, and on to Watchet (20 miles) on the coast of the Bristol Channel.

From Watchet the cyclist's path leads west along the coast, round Blue Anchor Bay to Minehead (6 miles) and on to Porlock (5 miles), famous as the home of the 'person from Porlock' who arrived unexpectedly at Coleridge's home and interrupted the composition of 'Kubla Khan', which was never completed.

Turn off a little west of here to tour on Exmoor and down a steep hill into the so-called Doone Country, named after R. D. Blackmore's novel, *Lorna Doone*. Go on to Exford and Simonsbath, through the Doone valley, a sparkling place, and then back down the A3223 on to another minor road to Oare where, in the church, Lorna was married and murdered. Blackmore's grandfather had been the vicar here. This is a circular trip, on minor roads, of some 25 miles. Turn west again, on the A39, for two pretty villages, Lynmouth and Lynton, pressing on along the coastal road to Combe Martin and Ilfracombe (12 miles). From here there is a pretty run south-west to Mortehoe, reached down a steep hill which seems to tip into the ocean, then around the sandy sweep of Morte Bay, past Woolacombe, and into the port of Barnstaple (17 miles) on the river Taw.

From here there are almost too many places to visit, but Bideford (9 miles) lies on the way west, and it is only a short diversion to see Westward Ho!, a Victorian resort, and the shipbuilding port at Appledore. From Bideford sweep west to Clovelly (11 miles), a very small village with cobbled streets dropping to the harbour, then ride out to Hartland Point for views of Lundy Island.

Now start the long ride into Cornwall on the A39, go past Bude and Boscastle to Arthur's castle at Tintagel (35 miles), a fairly stiff trip, often hilly and usually into the wind. From here take the B3314 to Port Isaac, less well known but very picturesque and full of narrow alleyways called drangs. Don't miss it.

Cut inland round the Camel estuary to Wadebridge, and follow the A39 and A3059 back to the coast at Newquay (25 miles), a tourist town and surfing centre. Crantock (2 miles), across the Gannel

Tintagel Castle.

Newquay, Cornwall

estuary, has delightful thatched colour-washed cottages, a fine church, St Carantoc, and a good pub, the Old Albion. Follow minor roads close to the coast to Perranporth (7 miles), then the coast road to St Ives (24 miles), best seen out of season and always crowded in summer. From here take the B3306 along the coast to Zennor (4 miles), a wild up-and-down road over the windswept moor, and on, pedalling hard to St Just, past Sennen Cove and out on to the breezy, rocky heights of Land's End (18 miles), the last of England.

I felt a great sense of relief at Land's End when I turned round and got that Atlantic wind at my back – perhaps because, on the day I was there, it was blowing a full gale from the west and the seas were huge and frightening. The wind blew me round the B3315 to Penzance (14 miles), for a quiet evening and a walk across the causeway to St Michael's Mount. There is plenty to see around Penzance, notably the pretty fishing villages of Mousehole and Marazion, but from here the cyclist's road lies inland, away from the coast. Leave on the A394 but turn off past Marazion for the B3280, heading up the rocky spine of Cornwall on minor roads to Truro, (33 miles), then on to the A390 for St Austell (14 miles). Here turn north on a very minor road to St Blazey (3 miles) and up to Lostwithiel, a small medieval town (8 miles) guarded to the north by the well-preserved castle of Restormel. From here the B3268 leads up to Bodmin (5 miles).

At Bodmin you leave the towns and villages behind and strike to the east across the open country of Bodmin Moor, on the road through St Neot, which has a fine church. Then ride on across the Moor to Bray

Shop (22 miles) on the B3257, and east again, out of Cornwall to the town of Tavistock in Devon. This is a marvellous day's ride of some 40 miles, wandering across this beautiful and little-travelled moor to the edge of another one, Dartmoor.

Tavistock lies on the western side of Dartmoor, that vast tract of rock, bog, gorse and heather which occupies most of central Devon, and here I might as well declare my preference for moorland and open country. Some people like the mountains but I like the sense of space and sky you get in the moors and the desert, or, in this case, across the wastes of Dartmoor.

From Tavistock the cyclist's road leads across the middle of Dartmoor to Princetown and Two Bridges (8 miles), then north-east to Mortonhampstead (12 miles), on a fairly rolling road, the B3212, the moor dotted on either side with rocky tors. Those with time on their hands can linger here and even ride south to Widecombe-in-the-Moor, where a fair is still held as in the old folksong, but our route presses on, still on the B3912, towards Exeter, though turning north after 7 miles to Crediton (6 miles).

From here the route heads east, but edging north all the time, and through open country to Cullompton, circling the Blackdown Hills to the south and turning north through a host of little villages up the B3170 into Taunton (27 miles). A large, pleasant, market town, Taunton is a good place to make a night stop. Leave by turning south on the A358, then fork left for Langport, and turn left again on to a minor road just after the turn, heading through North Curry and Strathe on the river Parrett. Follow this stream round to Langport (16 miles) before taking the B3153 for Somerton and Castle Cary (15 miles). Castle Cary is a pretty town, well worth a last look before taking the A371 north for Shepton Mallet (9 miles), then east on the A361 for 2 miles to Doulting, then north towards Bristol through the suburb of Keynsham (20 miles).

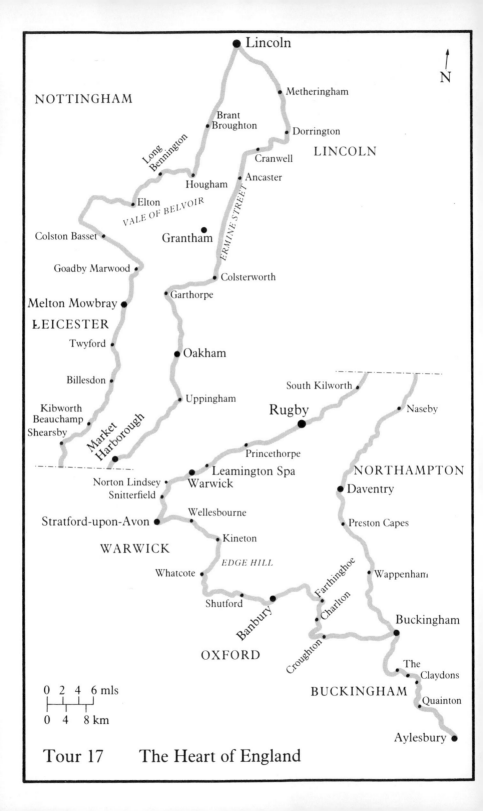

Tour 17   The Heart of England

TOUR 17

The Heart of England

All places, all airs, make unto me one country; I am in England,
everywhere, and under any meridian.
SIR THOMAS BROWNE, *Religio Medici*

Distance 405 miles

Time Two weeks

Counties Buckinghamshire, Warwickshire, Leicestershire, Nottinghamshire, Lincolnshire

Maps GT No.4 (Midlands)
National Series No.14 (Oxford), No.19 (Birmingham and Northampton), No.24 (Derby and Nottingham), No.30 (Lincoln), No.25 (Fenland)

Guidebooks *Shakespeare Country and the Cotswolds*, Vivian Bird (Ward Lock)
The Centre of England, Victor Skipp (Eyre Methuen)

Starting point Aylesbury

One of the main aims of this book is to discover, or rediscover, those parts of Britain which have slipped a little out of mind, or which are best seen on a cycle tour where the effort involved in getting there adds to the pleasures of arrival. To add diversity to these tours, too, cyclists have to visit places where most car-borne people don't go, and find a reason for going there; and so to the Shires.

The Shires really are the heart of England; they are not merely tourist areas which come alive for a few months in the year, but the backbone of the country, rich, heavily cultivated land, well forested, a cared-for place where the farmers still love to hunt over the fields where their forefathers have hunted for generations past. Among all this are scores of quiet villages, small market towns and many places of great beauty and historic interest. I can't think why more people don't go there.

OVERLEAF Leicestershire countryside, above Brauston.

Once I had settled on a tour of the Shires, the main problem was to skirt the sprawling industrial towns of the Midlands and those motorways and main roads which criss-cross the region, and find the minor roads, free from heavy traffic. Planning this tour was great fun, though it took a little time, and the original outline worked very well in practice. The terrain is moderate, so normal gearing is sufficient; there is no shortage of accommodation, mostly in bed and breakfasts, and on these minor roads the traffic is minimal, though naturally heavier than in more remote parts of the country. I should point out that I was frequently lost, and that the signposting is often abysmal. That hitch apart, this is a marvellous trip, and I commend it to you. It begins in Aylesbury, the county town of Buckinghamshire.

Aylesbury is a classic market town, if somewhat over-developed, with a ghastly administrative block in the centre, so after a look at John Hampden's statue in the main square and the old houses in the small streets round about take the A41 north. Turn right after 2 miles on the road for Quainton and the Claydons (10 miles), all small, pretty villages. Claydon House, a beautiful National Trust property, was once the home of the Verney family, one of whom was Charles I's Standard Bearer and died defending the King's banner at Edgehill.

From here it is a pleasant ride to the little town of Buckingham (8 miles), which has a lot of agreeable architecture, some fine inns and an interesting church. Leaving here, follow the A421 west for 4 miles and then take the B4031 for 8 miles before turning north through Charlton and Farthinghoe into the pleasant, broad, tree-lined streets of Banbury (10 miles), famous for its cross, its cakes and, once upon a time, the fervour of the Puritan religion, where:

> A Puritan hanged his cat
> on a Monday,
> For catching of a mouse
> on a Sunday.

Leave by the B4035, turning west through Shutford to the famous manor house, Compton Wynyates, before turning north-west to Whatcote and Kineton on the B4086 and into Stratford-on-Avon (28 miles) in Warwickshire.

Belvoir Castle.

Stratford is a famous place, and rightly so. See all the Shakespeare memorabilia before riding on, first up the A46 and then north-west on a minor road to Snitterfield and Norton Lindsey, and so into Warwick (12 miles). Warwick has a splendid castle and some marvellous medieval churches and inns, while Leamington Spa, 3 miles to the east, is an elegant Regency town with beautiful gardens. At least a day exploring these two towns would be enjoyable.

From here, head north-east on the B4453 across the arrow-like Roman Fosse Way and into Rugby (12 miles), famous for the public school where rugby football was invented, and Tom Browne studied. Dunchurch, 3 miles to the south, is a quiet little place, with stocks on the green; at the Lion Inn here Guy Fawkes' Gunpowder Plot was hatched in 1605.

Head north on the B5414, under the M6 and M1, into Leicestershire, skirting Husbands Bosworth (10 miles) and the delightful village of Arnsby, all the way up to Melton Mowbray. The route, always on minor roads, is a rural ride of around 50 miles, a good day's run from Rugby.

Melton Mowbray lies in Leicestershire, but close to the Nottinghamshire border, and is the centre of the great foxhunting region of the Midlands, as well as being famous for pies and Stilton cheese. It's an evocative English town, full of old inns. The sound of horses' hooves is heard everywhere, and if you met Dickens's Mr Pickwick and his friends you wouldn't be a bit surprised. It is a fine place to spend the night and drink a little English ale.

Leave Melton Mowbray on the A607, turning left after a mile for Goadby Marwood and then, north and west, for Colston Basset and the Vale of Belvoir. Colston Basset lies on the little river Smite, and is a noted centre for Stilton cheese as well as having a pleasant church, while the Vale of Belvoir, which you will ride up south to north, offers one of the finest landscapes in Britain. On the way north, towards Long Bennington (18 miles), veer east to Bottesford on the river Devon, a marvellous little-visited spot with a stone bridge over the river, a Norman market cross and such grim relics of the past as stocks and a whipping post.

From Long Bennington, which lies just in Lincolnshire, the route runs east to Hougham (3 miles), and then north along a river valley, the Brant, to the great city of Lincoln (20 miles), the most northern point on this tour and a very worthy objective. Seen from far off, across the plain, Lincoln rises like a beacon, calling the traveller on.

The city stands on a steep hill, crowned by the Norman cathedral, the third largest church in the country, which soars up above the surrounding countryside. It needs a full day to explore and enjoy the cathedral, the castle and the medieval wool merchants' houses, home of the weavers who made the famous Lincoln green cloth worn by Robin Hood and his followers.

Head south on the B1188 for some 14 miles to beyond Dorrington, then west on to the B1429, past the RAF College at Cranwell, and on to another great Roman road, Ermine Street, here the B6403. Follow it south, past Grantham to Colsterworth on the A1 (25 miles). Turn west here, take the B676 to Garthorpe, and from there follow a minor road south into Oakham (20 miles), on the western edge of Rutland Water. Oakham, once the county town of the now defunct Rutland, remains an elegant little place with a very fine parish church.

From here it is 6 miles on a minor road to Uppingham, another agreeable spot, where a minor road, the B664, runs south-west to Market Harborough (12 miles), on the Northamptonshire border, where Charles I held his last council before the disastrous battle at Naseby. Take the B4036 and ride south for 6 miles into Naseby, then go through West Haddon, over the M1, and into the little town of Daventry (12 miles), another unexpectedly attractive place. A hilltop town, Daventry was once a great coaching centre, which has left it with a number of fine inns and some splendid Georgian houses. It is well worth a night stop, but who, except cycle tourists, would think to visit Daventry today?

From Daventry you have a long last day riding south, always on minor roads, to Wappenham (21 miles), past Silverstone, and back through Buckingham (11 miles) to Aylesbury (17 miles). You will have enjoyed a delightful and very different tour into the true heartland of England, and the unspoilt country of the Shires.

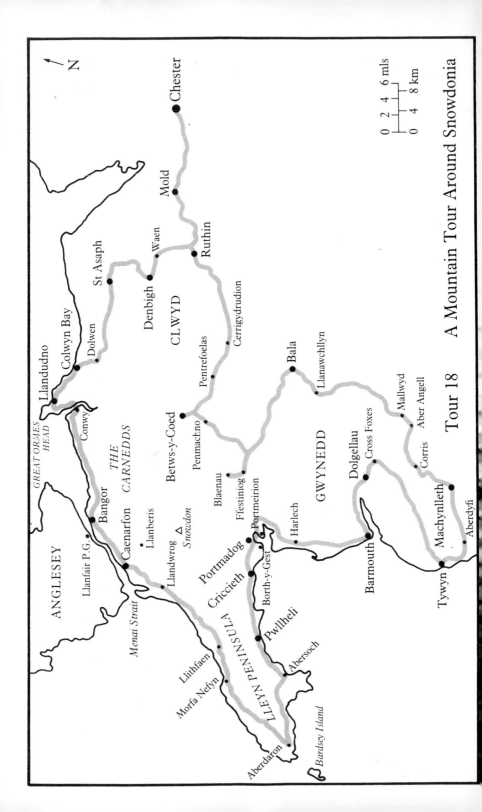

A Mountain Tour Around Snowdonia

Tour 18

TOUR 18

A Mountain Tour Around Snowdonia

All I heard him say of it was, that instead of bleak and barren mountains, there were green and fertile ones; and that one of the castles in Wales would contain all the castles he had seen in Scotland.
JAMES BOSWELL, *Life of Johnson*

Distance   450 miles

Time   Two or three weeks

Counties   Clwyd, Gwynedd

Maps   GT No.3 (Wales)
National Series No.28 (Manchester and Merseyside), No.27 (North Wales), No.22 (Mid-Wales)

Guidebooks   *Wales*, W. A. Poucher (Constable)
A Visitor's Guide to North Wales and Snowdonia, Colin Macdonald, (Moorland Publishing)

Starting point   Chester

Much of Snowdonia is now a National Park, a vast, sprawling, mountainous area long popular with walkers and climbers, a fact which, given enough minor roads, indicates that it will also be popular with those wandering cycle tourists who are not afraid of a few steep hills. North Wales is anyway a place apart, where the Welsh language is still widely spoken and the countryside still unspoiled. For that reason alone it is well worth visiting. Snowdonia is fairly compact and this tour explores the entire region from the Marches west to the tip of the Lleyn peninsula, on a journey where a lot of time is spent wandering on small mountain roads, climbing slowly to the cols and passes and soaking up the view.

There is plenty of accommodation, from comfortable hotels to camp sites, but the weather can be erratic and the terrain is mountainous, so this tour will probably appeal rather more to self-sufficient, hard riders, well equipped for cycle touring, than to those

OVERLEAF The winding road to Penmachno.

181

who like to meander gently across a green and rolling landscape. Good map reading will be helpful, and those who like to mix their cycling trips with a little hill walking, as many do, will find this the ideal tour, though they should be prepared to allow a full three weeks. As usual, pre-trip research has found places worth visiting off the metalled track, and this trip begins in the city of Chester, a short ride from the Marches of Wales.

Leave Chester (see Tour 4) by the A55 and A494, heading west and a little south for 38 miles into Ruthin, a typical border town full of black and white Tudor buildings and an excellent church. Take the B5429 from here, north, through Waen to Denbigh (10 miles), which has a ruined castle, then up to see the smallest cathedral in Britain at St Asaph (6 miles); it dates back in parts to 537. From here the B5381 runs west and leads up to the coast at Colwyn Bay (16 miles).

The North Wales coast between Prestatyn and Llandudno is a popular tourist area, with the Snowdonia range looming up to the south, so follow the coast to the west on A roads to Llandudno (9 miles) for a ride round the Great Ormes Head, then to Conwy (6

LEFT The valley of Nant Gwynant, west of Blaenau.
ABOVE Snowdon from Capel Curig.

185

miles), which has one of the finest of those great castles built by Edward I to subdue the Welsh, and on to Bangor (15 miles). Bangor is a great starting-off place for outdoor lovers heading up into Snowdonia, but first cross the Menai Strait on to the island of Anglesey for a brief visit to the village of Llanfair P.G., 2 miles west of the Menai Bridge. Its full name, from which one can see the need for the abbreviation, is Llanfairpwllgwyngyllgogerychwyrndrobwll-llantysiliogogogoch. Castle lovers can ride north from here to see the fortress at Beaumaris (8 miles) before returning over the bridge to the mainland.

Return to Gwynedd and take the A487 to Caernarfon (9 miles), which has another thirteenth-century castle. From here the B4086 leads to Llanberis (6 miles), where the Snowdon Mountain Railway can transport you to the summit at 3560 ft. Those who want to walk or climb will find Llanberis a good base. Wise travellers will leave their bikes here and spend a few days walking in the Welsh mountains; the Glyders, Glyder-fach and Glyder-fawr, lie to the north of the Llanberis Pass, and those who ride round to Capel Curig and west down the A5 back to Bangor (33 miles) can try another fine range of hills, the Carnedds. Many peaks hereabouts top the 3000 ft (1000 m) mark, and the hill walking is superb.

From Caernarfon set out down the Lleyn peninsula, an area often overlooked by visitors to North Wales. Take the minor road to Llandwrog (5 miles), then the A499, B4417 and B4413 down to Aberdaron, right at the western foot of the Lleyn peninsula (35 miles), a good day's run. Aberdaron lies at the bottom of a steep hill, facing out to the bay, and a little to the west lies Bardsey Island, which is worth visiting.

Turn here, across the peninsula, on small roads close to the coast, to Abersoch (7 miles), a very attractive fishing port and sailing centre, and then take the A499 to the resort of Pwllheli and on to Criccieth (16 miles), which has another great castle and is the epitome of a small Welsh town. East of here lies Porthmadog (3 miles), and a mile to the south the beautiful little fishing village of Borth-y-Gest, which has a fine beach framed by woods and hills, and on to another popular tourist spot, the village of Portmeirion, the attractive if unusual creation of the architect Sir Clough Williams-Ellis.

Head south from here, down the A496, to arrive at Harlech (10 miles), with a castle made famous by a Welsh song, and on down the coast for another 10 miles into the resort of Barmouth. Here turn up the Mawddach estuary for 9 miles to Dolgellau, then ride on a minor road to Cross Foxes (3 miles). Head south-west on the A487 and B4405 for Tywyn (21 miles) on the coast, and then go south to Aberdyfi (4 miles) on the Dyfi estuary, a neat little place with a golf course, a wide beach beyond the dunes, and high hills behind – a good place to stop for a day. Turn inland here for 10 miles to Machynlleth, then head north into the hills, to Corris (4 miles), which lies in a narrow valley and is surrounded by green slopes and grey slate quarries. Take the very minor road east to Aber Angell (5 miles) and then north to Mallwyd (2 miles), a busy place in the valley of the Dyfi.

You are now getting back into the heart of Snowdonia, and after Mallwyd go north for a mile on the A470, then veer north on a steep, narrow road up beside the river Dyfi and over the hill to Llanawchllyn (15 miles), a straggling village beside the lake, and the southern terminal of the Bala Lake Railway. Follow the lake up to Bala itself (15 miles) on the B4403.

From Bala the route lies west, to the A4212 junction with the B4391, which you should follow to Ffestiniog (18 miles) where, after a brief visit to Blaenau (3 miles), further up the valley, take the B4391 and the B4407 and then turn north on a minor road to Penmachno (15 miles), and the river Conwy. Penmachno lies on the river Machno at a gap in the open moorland, which the road crosses into the little town of Betws-y-Coed (5 miles).

From Betws turn east again for the long final run, first on the A5, a fairly major road. Turn off after 12 miles on to the B5105, which runs north and east across the mountains, back into Ruthin (15 miles), a fine ride with which to end this tour.

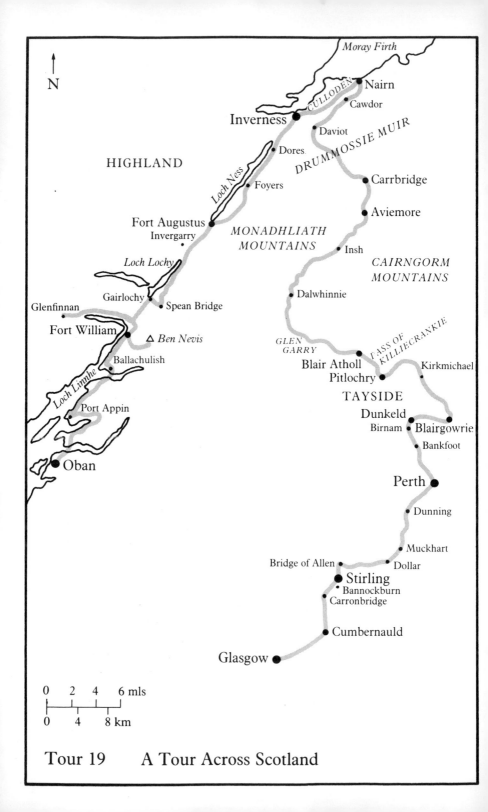

Tour 19　A Tour Across Scotland

TOUR 19

A Tour Across Scotland

Farewell, old Scotia's bleak domains,
Far dearer than the torrid plains.
ROBERT BURNS, *'The Farewell'*

Distance   458 miles

Time   Two weeks

Regions   Strathclyde, Highland, Tayside

Maps   GT No.7 (South West Scotland), No.9 (North West Scotland), No.10 (North East Scotland), No.8 (South East Scotland)
National Series No.47 (Oban and Mull), No.50 (Arisaig and Locharber), No.55 (Inverness and Moray), No.51 (Aviemore and Grampians), No.48 (Pitlochry and Trossachs), No.45 (Mid Scotland)

Guidebooks   *The Highlands of Scotland*, W. A. Poucher (Constable)
The Highlands and Islands of Scotland, J. Carter (Batsford)
Discover Scotland, Bryn Frank (U & B Publications)
The Scottish Highlands, J. A. Lister (Bartholomew)

Starting point   Oban

Having crossed England in Tour 11, it seemed only fair and reasonable to make a similar tour across my native Scotland, but there was a problem. Scotland is a sparsely populated country and there are few minor roads in the Highlands or, to be even more exact, few minor Highland roads which are not dead ends. Most of the roads, as a glance at the map will reveal, run north–south, and travelling east–west on minor roads is practically impossible without long diversions, for most of the roads lead up into the glens and stop abruptly. In the end any trans-Scotland trip has to use A class roads. In practice this is less of a problem than one might suppose, for even the A roads are, at least by more urban standards, very empty, so that this trip was less

OVERLEAF The Glenfinnan Memorial on Loch Shiel.

plagued by traffic than I had originally feared.

There is plenty of accommodation, but a tent and sleeping bag would not go amiss. Scottish weather is unreliable so take your waterproofs and hope for good weather, which is actually quite common. The distances are vast by British standards generally, and the countryside is often desolate, but those who like the thought of wandering in the Highlands will enjoy this long but always interesting tour, which begins in the western port of Oban, easily reached from Glasgow on the West Highland Line.

Begin this tour by cycling north from Oban up the coast, on the A85 and A828, into Port Appin, riding beside Loch Linnhe to the bridge at Ballachulish (34 miles), and up to the true start of this Scottish traverse at Fort William (15 miles), no beauty spot, but in a splendid setting. Do not leave this rather touristy little town without riding up the minor road to the foot of Ben Nevis (5 miles), or taking the A830 west on a day ride to Glenfinnan and back (24 miles), where Bonnie Prince Charlie raised his standard in 1745. Head north-west for the Great Glen; a minor road, the B8004, will prove useful, running beside the attractive Caledonian Canal to Gairlochy and then east to Spean Bridge (11 miles). Those who are interested can see the Commando Memorial here before taking the A82 beside Loch Lochy for the ride past Invergarry to Fort Augustus (23 miles) on the southern edge of Loch Ness. Much of this road lies beside the Caledonian Canal.

The A82 runs to the north of the loch, and takes most of the traffic, so take the A862 for a stiff climb up to the viewpoint, and then the B852 to Foyers (12 miles), which follows one of General Wade's military roads beside the lake all the way to Dores (14 miles). Keep a sharp look out over the loch in case the monster puts in an appearance! Foyers, where the military road begins, is a pretty spot, with a great waterfall dropping a hundred feet down the hillside, and there is a Loch Ness Monster Information Bureau on the lakeside. General Wade built this road in the 1730s, and if it seems a rough ride today remember the old rhyme:

> If you had seen this before it was made,
> You would raise up your hands, and bless General Wade.

This happy thought ignores the fact that the main purpose of his roads was to subdue the Highland clans.

From Dores the A862 runs on into Inverness (8 miles), a large, attractive town, the capital of the Highlands and well worth exploring. A little to the south, on the B9006, lies Drummossie Muir, where at Culloden, in 1746, Prince Charlie and his Highland army were defeated and the Jacobite cause extinguished for ever. The B9006 leads on to Cawdor (12 miles), whose castle is the seat of the Earls of Cawdor, the place where Duncan was murdered by Macbeth. From here the road leads on to the coast of the Moray Firth at Nairn (8 miles), completing this traverse of Scotland from sea to sea. Fortunately you still have to get home, so more can be seen of the Highlands on the way.

From Nairn, return west across Drummossie to Daviot (23 miles) on the A9, and follow this road south across the Monadhliath Mountains to Carrbridge (28 miles) and the valley of the river Spey at Aviemore (7 miles). The Spey Valley is famous for fishing and whisky, and Aviemore, a modern resort best known for its skiing, is an unusual sight in the Highlands, although the skiing actually takes place some miles away on the slopes of Cairngorm. The cyclist's path heads south and west, on the B970 to Spey Bridge (18 miles), skirting Cairngorm and the other peaks of the Grampians, on to the A9 and over Badenoch into Tayside and Glengarry and round to Blair Atholl (30 miles), at the foot of Glen Tilt. The scenery is marvellous all along this route, and after Blair Atholl a steep climb leads up to the famous Pass of Killiecrankie and then down to the agreeable little town of Pitlochry (7 miles), home of a popular summer festival.

At Pitlochry turn east on the A924 to Kirkmichael in Strathardle, if only for a meal at the beautiful Log Cabin Hotel, where cyclists are always very welcome, and then on to the Blairgowrie (25 miles), before turning west for 12 miles to Dunkeld and Birnam. From Birnam take the minor road to Bankfoot (6 miles) and then the A9 to Perth (11 miles), once the capital of Scotland. It remains an attractive town on the river Tay and contains the museum of the Black Watch regiment. Two miles to the north lies the Palace of Scone; Edward I sacked it in 1296 and stole the Pillow of Jacob stone, which now lies beneath the Coronation Chair in Westminster Abbey.

Take the B9112 and B934 out of Perth to Dunning (8 miles), and then the B934 again to Muckhart (13 miles), from which the A91 leads on to Dollar, Bridge of Allan, and so into Stirling (27 miles). This is the gateway to the Highlands and Stirling Castle, which contains the

The Cairngorms.

Loch Aline and the Cairngorms.

regimental museum of the Argyll and Sutherland Highlanders and stands high on the rock above the town, has been both the lock and the key. There is a lot to see in and around Stirling, so it justifies a full day as the end of this tour approaches. A little to the north lies the memorial to William Wallace, the fourteenth-century Scots patriot. It is said that you can see seven battlefields from the ramparts of Stirling, and the most famous of them all is surely Bannockburn, where Robert Bruce defeated Edward II in 1314, which lies just to the south. There is a museum on the battlefield.

Leaving Stirling, ride past Bannockburn and pick up the quiet road for Carronbridge. This will take you back into Glasgow through the town of Cumbernauld (36 miles), and the end of this tour.

TOUR 20

The End-to-End –
Land's End to John O' Groats

Every region excelleth all others in some peculiar rarity, which may be termed extraordinary, though otherwise most common in its own place.
SAMUEL PURCHAS, *Purchas his Pilgrim*

Distance   1,100 miles

Time   Three weeks

Maps   GT No.1 (West Country), No.4 (Midlands), No.5 (East Anglia), No.6 (North England), No.8 (South East Scotland), No.10 (North East Scotland)

Starting point   Land's End

This ride is a challenge. Any cycle ride of this distance, which you aim to complete within three weeks, must be a challenge, and when the journey has to be made from bottom left to top right of a very crowded country the problems are compounded by traffic and towns, by deep estuaries, by motorways, by hills and by a host of lesser obstacles, both man-made and natural.

It has to be understood that though the End-to-End is a popular ride, there is no *official* route. The *recognized* route runs via Gloucester, Preston and Gretna Green, and totals some 850 miles but the only fixed points are at Land's End and John O'Groats, and those who start at one end and reach the other have done the End-to-End, by whichever route they choose to take. Some map out the shortest way they can find, and burn up the distance in a couple of days, and if that's what they enjoy, good luck to them. Others choose a direct route, but take their time over it, content with simply getting from one end of the country to the other. Personally I have chosen to visit some of the interesting places which lie along the way. This tour is longer than other End-to-End routes, but I believe the extra distance is worth it, although on a ride of over a thousand miles it pays to cut the corners here and there. For this reason I have chosen to concentrate here more on the planning than on descriptions of the roads, the scenery, and the places en route, since much of this has been covered in the other tours which this book describes.

The End-to-End is the Great British Bike Ride, as John Potter of Bike Events so aptly calls it, and those who are thinking of attempting it should give some thought to the following points:

1. The best route is south to north, which takes advantage of any prevailing wind. The start at Land's End is, for most of the population anyway, much closer than the remote north-east of Scotland, and you may spend less time in getting there.

2. You should be fit and your machine in good order. The required average here is 50 miles a day, and any prolonged breakdown of bike or rider cannot easily be made up.

3. Plan your route in advance and stick to it, for you can waste hours poring over maps at windy crossroads.

4. While the choice of route depends entirely on the rider, give a thought to avoiding hills and major conurbations. My route uses the eastern side of the country for both these reasons, and even if it is longer than a more direct route north from Bath, it is a good deal less demanding.

5. My route often incorporates parts of previous tours, which proved most useful, not least because in knowing the way, and where to stop, I could take my time, ride later in the day and spend less time map reading. I also used some short cuts I missed on previous occasions.

6. It is a very long tour, but resist the temptation to ride half the distance in the first two days. Let the daily distances increase as your fitness improves and as the terrain permits.

The End-to-End route given here can be plotted on six GT maps. For ease of reference, therefore, I have broken this tour into five stages, which would-be End-to-End riders can mark out on their own maps. Anyone attempting the End-to-End should re-read the introductory sections, because good planning is essential.

STAGE 1 – Land's End to Bath: GT map No.1 (West Country)

Distance: 266 miles

Much of this stage follows the West of England tour (Tour 16). The railhead is at Penzance, 10 miles from Land's End, so the main points on the road are Land's End, Truro, St Austell, Bodmin, then across

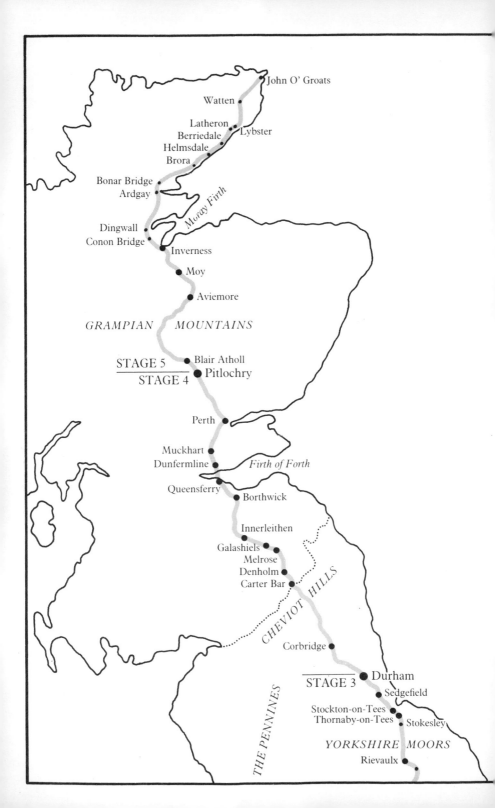

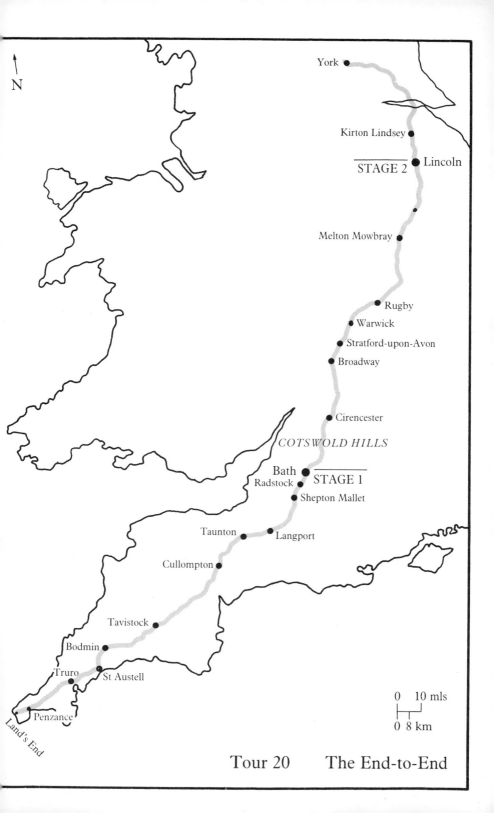

N

York

Kirton Lindsey
STAGE 2 Lincoln

Melton Mowbray

Rugby
Warwick
Stratford-upon-Avon
Broadway

Cirencester

COTSWOLD HILLS

Bath STAGE 1
Radstock
Shepton Mallet

Taunton Langport

Cullompton

Tavistock

Bodmin
Truro St Austell

Penzance
Land's End

0   10 mls
0   8 km

Tour 20   The End-to-End

Bodmin Moor to Tavistock. Then ride over Dartmoor, to skirt Exeter, and up to Cullompton. Go east to Churchingford, then north to Taunton and Langport. From there, cycle up the Fosse Way to Shepton Mallet and then, via Radstock, into Bath, a good place for a first day off. Note the Fosse Way, for by some curious historical fact which can hardly be an accident, many parts of this End-to-End route follow those ancient arrow-like Roman roads. As always, though, in plotting your route choose minor roads whenever possible.

STAGE 2 – Bath to Lincoln: GT map No.4 (Midlands)

Distance: 207 miles

Those End-to-End riders interested in a speedy trip would travel a more direct route from Bath to the Scottish Border, but as a glance at a topographical map will quickly reveal this involves crossing the Cotswolds, the industrial Midlands, the Peak District, parts of the Yorkshire Dales, and a host of lesser hills and industrial centres. I am less courageous and, besides, some attractive places lie further east.

Going out of Bath to the north, cross the M4, then go east to Stanton St Quintan on the A429 and north on this to Cirencester and on to Broadway, on minor roads whenever possible. They are faster, quieter and much safer. Then ride north to Stratford-upon-Avon, on much of the route followed on the Heart of England Tour (Tour 17), through Warwick, Rugby and Melton Mowbray, off that tour briefly to skirt the Vale of Belvoir to the east, joining up on the valley of the Brant from Marston, north of Grantham, and so into Lincoln, another good place to rest and look around if time permits.

STAGE 3 – Lincoln to Durham: GT maps No.5 (Midlands) and No.6 (North England)

Distance: 177 miles

Veering east, skirt the Pennines and take a good minor road, the B1398, which leads north from Lincoln to Kirton-in-Lindsey, lying a little west of the Roman Ermine Street. A major obstacle is looming

OPPOSITE ABOVE A Cotswold drove road.
BELOW The Cheviot Hills near Carter Bar.

up ahead, the river Humber, which offers only two helpful crossings, at Hull and at Goole further east. The choice is yours, but I chose the new Humber Bridge and then took the A1079 for York. This route has the advantage of being more interesting and it also avoids the East Midlands motorway network.

From York the route strikes north on the B1363, crossing the Yorkshire Moors and Dales Tour (Tour 7), and then offers a marvellous ride up Bilsdale on the B1257 from Rievaulx to Thornaby-on-Tees, Stockton-on-Tees (the only snag), then Sedgefield and, on a minor road through Trimdon, into Durham for the next pause on this journey.

STAGE 4 – Durham to Pitlochry: GT map No.8 (South East Scotland)

Distance: 199 miles

From Durham start to edge back towards the north-west, taking the A691 to Headgrave, and then riding on the B6309 to Ebchester. Stay on the B6309 and cross the Tyne on the A68, which the route follows, crossing into Scotland at Carter Bar in the Cheviots. At Carter Bar take the A6088 for 8 miles and then fork right on a minor road to Denholm and so north on the B6359 to Melrose and Galashiels, where this route picks up the A72, west for Innerleithen. From here the B709 runs due north to the A7 and so, by Dalkeith, into Edinburgh. Here again, the problem is a great indentation, the Firth of Forth, but take the bull by the horns and cross by the A90 road bridge from Queensferry into Dunfermline, following the A823 up to the delightfully named Yetts of Muckhart. Then, searching as always for minor roads, take the B934 to Perth, where this stage joins Tour 19, though heading in the reverse direction, up to Pitlochry.

STAGE 5 – Pitlochry to John O'Groats: GT map No.10 (North East Scotland)

Distance: 233 miles

One of the advantages of using overlapping maps on a very long tour like this is that it helps to avoid that sinking feeling of doom which occurs when you unfold yet another map and see that after days on the road, there still seems a long way to go. Then you realize that you are already a few miles up the map, and feel a little better.

The route from Pitlochry follows the route of Tour 19, all the way up to Inverness, a distance of about 90 miles and a marvellous run over a good road, the A9. Owing to the terrain, this main road is the only practical route, but there are a number of B roads which run parallel to the A road and can be taken.

From Inverness the route crosses the Moray Firth by ferry to Northkessock, and follows the B9162 and the A9 to Dingwall, then goes up beside the Cromarty Firth for 6 miles to the A836, which cuts north over a wild stretch of country to Bonar Bridge at the head of Dornoch Firth. Here a very minor road runs over the moors to Loch Fleet, and then the A9, that persistent road, reappears beside the North Sea and sweeps north through Brora, Helmsdale and Berriedale for some 65 miles to Latheron and Lybster, from where another minor road cuts across the neck of the peninsula to Watten (18 miles). Then ride on the B870 to the north for a further 16 miles out to the Pentland Firth at Gill Bay, only 3 miles from the end of this journey at John O'Groats.

Loch Leven, Inverness.

Appendix 1
Cycling and Camping Organizations

The Association of Lightweight Campers, 11 Grosvenor Place, London SW1 0EY (tel. 01–828 1012)

British Cycling Federation, 16 Upper Woburn Place, London WC1H 0QE (tel. 01–387 9320)

Cyclists' Touring Club, Cotterell House, 69 Meadrow, Godalming, Surrey, GU7 3HS (tel. 04868 7217)

Rough-Stuff Fellowship, 4 Archray Avenue, Callander, Central, FK17 8JZ (tel. 0877 30104)

Youth Hostels Association (England and Wales), National Office, Trevelyan House, 8 St Stephen's Hill, St Albans, Hertfordshire, AL1 2DY (tel. 0727 55215)

Scottish Youth Hostels Association, National Office, 7 Glebe Crescent, Stirling, FK8 2JA (tel. 0786 2821)

Appendix 2
Suggested Cycle Touring Kit List

The amount of clothing and equipment you carry depends on the tour you have in mind. In every case, the less you take the better, for it all adds weight. Everything should fit easily and securely into the panniers and handlebar bag.

General

Chequebook and card
Credit cards

Cycle and personal insurance
Camera/film

Clothing

Worn:
Shirt
Shorts/trousers
Socks
Underwear
Shoes
Gloves
Sunglasses
Handkerchief

Carried : Spare shirt

Pullover
Shorts/trousers
2 pairs socks
2 sets underwear
1 set thermal underwear
Spare shoes/clothing
Rainproofs
Hat
Handkerchiefs

Toilet and Medical Equipment

Lip salve
Sun cream
Soap
Towel
Shaving gear/cosmetics
Shampoo
First-aid kit

Camping and Cooking

Tent
Sleeping bag
Sleeping pad
Stove
Cookset
Knife, fork, spoon
Bottle/tin opener

Information

Maps
Notebook, with list of addresses,
    telephone numbers of hotels, B
    and Bs, bike shops etc.

Cycle Tools and Spares

Puncture repair outfit
1 spare tyre (cover)
2 spare tubes
3 spare spokes
1 (rear) brake cable
1 (rear) gear cable
Assorted tools
Allan keys, pliers
Lock and chain
Shock cords

Appendix 3
British Tourist Boards

English Tourist Board, 4 Grosvenor Gardens, London SW1W 0DU (tel. 01–730 3400)

Scottish Tourist Board, 23 Ravelston Terrace, Edinburgh EH4 3EU (tel. 031–332 2433)

Wales Tourist Board, Brunel House, 2 Fitzalan Road, Cardiff, CF2 1UY (tel. 0222 499909)

British Tourist Authority (for enquiries from overseas), 64 St James's Street, London SW1A 1NF (tel. 01–629 9191)

Cumbria Tourist Board (covering Cumbria), Ellerthwaite, Windermere, Cumbria, LA23 2AQ (tel. 096 62 4444/7)

Northumbria Tourist Board (covering Cleveland, Durham, Northumberland and Tyne and Wear), 9 Osborne Terrace, Jesmond, Newcastle-upon-Tyne, NE2 1NT (tel. 0632 817744)

North West Tourist Board (covering Cheshire, Greater Manchester, Lancashire, Merseyside and the High Peak District of Derbyshire), The Last Drop Village, Bromley Cross, Bolton, Lancashire, BL7 9PZ (tel. 0204 591511)

Yorkshire and Humberside Tourist Board, 312 Tadcaster Road, York, North Yorkshire, YO2 2HF (tel. 0904 707961)

Heart of England Tourist Board (covering Gloucestershire, Hereford and Worcester, Shropshire, Staffordshire, Warwickshire and West Midlands), PO Box 15, Worcester, WR1 2JT (tel. 0905 29511)

East Midlands Tourist Board (covering Derbyshire, Leicestershire, Lincolnshire, Northamptonshire and Nottinghamshire), Exchequergate, Lincoln, LN2 1PZ (tel. 0522 31521/3)

Thames and Chilterns Tourist Board (covering Oxfordshire, Berkshire, Bedfordshire, Buckinghamshire and Hertfordshire), 8 Market Place, Abingdon, Oxfordshire, OX14 3UD (tel. 0253 22711)

East Anglia Tourist Board (covering Cambridgeshire, Essex, Norfolk and Suffolk), 14 Museum Street, Ipswich, Suffolk, IP1 1HU (tel. 0473 214211)

London Tourist Board (covering Greater London area), 26 Grosvenor Gardens, London SW1W 0DU (tel. 01–730 0791)

West Country Tourist Board (covering Avon, Cornwall, Devon, western Dorset, Somerset, Wiltshire and Isles of Scilly), Trinity Court, 37 Southernhay East, Exeter, Devon, EX1 1QS (tel. 0392 76351)

Southern Tourist Board (covering Hampshire, eastern Dorset and Isle of Wight), Town Hall Centre, Leigh Road, Eastleigh, Hampshire, SO5 4DE (tel. 0703 616027)

South East Tourist Board (covering Sussex, Kent, Surrey), Cheviot House, 4–6 Monson Road, Tunbridge Wells, Kent, TN1 1NH (tel. 0892 40766)

British Tourist Authority Overseas Offices

Australia 171 Clarence Street, Sydney, NSW 2000 (tel. 02–29 8627)

Canada 94 Cumberland Street, Suite 600, Toronto, Ontario, M5R 3N3 (tel. 416–925 6326)

South Africa 7th Floor, JBS Building, 107 Commissioner St, Johannesburg 2001, PO Box 6256 (tel. 11–29 6770)

Denmark Møntergade 3, DK-1116 København (tel. 01–12 07 93)

Italy Via S. Eufemia 5, 00187 Roma (tel. 678 4998 or 678 5548)

Sweden Malmskillnadsg 42, 1st Floor (for callers). Box 7293, S-103 90 Stockholm (for mail) (tel. 08–21 24 44)

USA John Hancock Center, Suite 3320, 875 N. Michigan Avenue, Chicago, Illinois 60611 (tel. 312–757 0490)

Plaza of the Americas, 750 North Tower, Lb346, Dallas, Texas 75201 (tel. 214–748 2279)

612 South Flower St, Los Angeles, Ca 90017 (tel. 213–623 8196)

3rd Floor, 40 West 57th St, New York, NY 10019 (tel. 212–581 4700)

Bibliography

General

Historic Britain (Robert Nicolson)
The AA Book of British Villages (Reader's Digest)
The Past All Around Us (Reader's Digest)
The Old Country ed. Audrey Butler (Dent)
Coming Down the Wye Robert Gibbins (Dent)
Holy Places of the British Isles William Anderson (Ebury Press)
The Sunday Times Book of the Countryside (Macdonald and Jane's)
The Ramblers' and Cyclists' Bed and Breakfast Guide (Cyclists' Touring Club)
The Best Bed and Breakfast in the World, Sigourney Wells (UKHM Publishing Co. and East Woods Press, USA)
Traveller's Britain Arthur Eperon (Pan)
Treasures of Britain (Automobile Association)
The Age of Chivalry Arthur Bryant (Collins)
Through Britain on Country Roads Peter Brereton (Arthur Barker)
A Pictorial History of English Architecture John Betjeman (John Murray)
Pevsner's *Buildings of Britain* series (Penguin)
Poems and Places, ed. Geoffrey Grigson (Faber)
AA Guide to Castles in Wales (AA/WTB Publications)
The Pilgrim Way John Adair (Thames and Hudson)

Cycling

Three Men on the Bummel Jerome K. Jerome (Penguin)
Fat Man on a Roman Road Tom Vernon (Michael Joseph)
Fat Man on a Bicycle Tom Vernon (Michael Joseph)
Adventure Cycling Tim Hughes (Blandford)
The CTC Route Guide to Cycling in Britain and Ireland C. Gausden and N. Crane (Penguin)
Weekend Cycling C. Gausden (Hamlyn)
Bicycle Touring in Europe K. and G. Hawkins (Pantheon Books, New York)
Cycling Jeanne Mackenzie (Oxford University Press)
The Young Cyclist's Handbook Ken Evans (Hamlyn)
Bike Touring Raymond Bridge (Sierra Club, USA)
Bike-Packing Robin Adshead (Oxford Illustrated Press)
Cycling in Europe N. Crane (Oxford Illustrated Press)
International Cycling Guide (1983) (Tantivy Press)

Cycles and Cycle Maintenance

The Penguin Bicycle Handbook Rob Van der Plas (Penguin)
Richard's Bicycle Book Richard Ballantine (Pan)
The Bicycle Buyer's Bible (The Bicycle Co-operative)
Freewheeling: The Bicycle Camping Book Raymond Bridge (Stackpole Books, USA)

Cycling Magazines

Bicycle (monthly). 89–91 Bayham Street, London NW1 (tel. 01–482 2040).
Bicycle Times (monthly). 26 Commercial Buildings, Dunston, Gateshead, NE11 9AA (tel. 0632 608113)
Cycletouring (bi-monthly). Cyclists' Touring Club, Cotterell House, 69 Meadrow, Godalming, Surrey, GU7 3HS (tel. 04868 7217)
Cycling (weekly). Surrey House, 1 Throwley Way, Sutton, Surrey, SM1 4QQ (tel. 01–643 8040)
Cycling World (monthly). Andrew House, 2A Granville Road, Sidcup, Kent DA14 4BN